The Far-Out Saints of the Jesus Communes

The Far-Out Saints

A FIRSTHAND REPORT

AND INTERPRETATION OF THE

JESUS PEOPLE MOVEMENT

of the Jesus Communes

By HILEY H. WARD

ASSOCIATION PRESS, NEW YORK

THE FAR-OUT SAINTS OF THE JESUS COMMUNES

Copyright © 1972 by Hiley H. Ward
Association Press, 291 Broadway, New York, N.Y. 10007

International Standard Book Number: 0-8096-1842-7
Library of Congress Catalog Card Number: 73-189010

Library of Congress Cataloging in Publication Data

Ward, Hiley H.
    The far-out saints of the Jesus communes.

    Bibliography: p.
    1. Youth—Religious life. I. Title.
BV4531.2.W35   248'.83   73-189010
ISBN 0-8096-1842-7

Printed in the United States of America

To my children
Dianne, Carolee, Marceline, Laurel

Contents

1

"Saints": A Clue
to the Movement

The frame house above a hill of steps in north Seattle was un-
marked and dim in a descending mist near midnight. Unlike many
of the shared homes of the young people who are coming off drugs
and alienation from home and family, the signless house was indis-
tinguishable as a place of God. Inside, there were a few Bibles,
but they were not in use, since this was a time for work or sleep.
The seven young men all work either day or night shifts around
town. I learned later that their main passion is to conduct a feed-in
twice a week for the poor at the nearby Blessed Sacrament and St.
Joseph Catholic parishes.

As I waited for the leader, Carl Furioso, a fuzzy-haired former
Ann Arbor, Michigan, yippie, another house member, Mike Shoe-
maker, twenty-three, said something that stuck with me all during
the rest of my travels among the houses of the Jesus People, as
the new, enthusiastic young converts are called at this moment
in history (at first they were called Jesus Freaks, reflecting the
link many of them formerly had with the dropout drug counterculture).

In the quiet living room, Mike said, "God is going to bring some
saints out of the Jesus movement. He's got some pretty holy
people."

Saints?

Could it be that God's children of the new wave, with their radiant, innocent faces, shouting, "Oh, wow, Jesus loves you!" are saints in his eyes? Why not?

It became a useful definitive concept. "Saints" allows for the great experiential element in the movement. Saintliness is a corrective to the barrenness in liberal and orthodox Christianity. Saintliness allows for a celebrative faith, one of joy and conviction. It allows for a sense of, or seeking of, mystical union. Saintliness allows for concern for one's fellow man.

When you drop in on Jesus communes in old jeans, tennis shoes, old shirt or sweater, as I did in researching for this book, you become a part of their lives. They are not on stage. You are living in a family—and families—of Jesus.

Watch them as they pray at the bedside, at the table, on the floor—sometimes prostrate on the floor, more often than not waving arms. "Oh, Jesus, thank you, we just thank you, Lord Jesus . . . amen . . . hallelujah. . . ."

They are barefoot; they sit on the floor; a little morning light comes into an upper room of a duplex or into a plain parlor on the main floor beneath scattered posters that reflect their joy and love for Jesus.

Somehow the distance between them and Jesus—or whatever eternal or internal force men can relate to in their deeper, selfless, reflective moments—seems very short.

The Jesus People are close to God . . . or something. (I am sure that Andrew Greeley, the sociologist and director of the Center for American Pluralism at the National Opinion Research Center at the University of Chicago, was right in pointing out to me that it is too early in life to make that comparison—of Jesus People as saints. Yet not all saintliness has to await recognition via the centuries-long saint-determining system devised by the Roman Catholics and others.)

If saints are calm and radiant, then consider beautiful Helen Harwood, twenty, from Beraiah House, Costa Mesa, California. See the calmness she maintains as a crew-cut, knobby young man just out of a mental institution begins scary talk much too close to her as she visits a sloppy Berkeley Jesus commune. She does not move a muscle; her faith envelops her.

Or if joy is a measure of sainthood, consider Sister Bethia in the very tight, hard-to-crash, controversial Children of God commune in Los Angeles, since closed after the Children's hassle with benefactor Fred Jordan. Watch her as the home-style hard-rock band with a flute lets go. She jumps and dances on the couch, joins the group snake dance, smiles and sings and shouts.

I

Carolyn Sim must surely be one of God's saints.

You sit and talk with her at length—or rather listen at length—as she is encouraged to tell her story, over candles, in a rather heavy, dull and uninspiring Jesus coffee house in Vancouver, British Columbia.

Carolyn's story is best seen and heard in contrast, just as the lives of the saints of the past stood out in contrast to cruelty, pomposity and materialism—St. Sebastian dying from Roman arrows; Joan of Arc at the stake; St. Francis living, but giving all; the recently canonized African saints remaining true and pure in their morals. The saints are always risking, unturned in loyalty, giving, always giving, always something.

"I have no silver and gold, but I give you what I have." (Acts 3:6).

And it may not be more than a glow, over a softer candle glow.

I entered the Shepherd's Call Coffee House in Vancouver with tall, slim Robin, twenty-two, a lab technician, who was interested in looking in on some of the Jesus People in Vancouver simply because she had heard of these new fundamentalist youths and their zeal for Jesus.

She, however, was not impressed with their coffee house. Or at least, she was not until she listened to the incredible Carolyn, the bright-eyed miss from central Canada, who had been through hell.

Robin was right. The Shepherd's Call Coffee House, run by the Jesus People Army (one of the offshoots of a Seattle program), was a very sad place.

"It looks like a dope anonymous meeting," said Robin, as she sat down among the dreary deadbeats. Somebody brought cupcakes and hot chocolate just before the kitchen closed its door at midnight.

"I can't see sitting in this place drinking hot chocolate by stupid candles," said Robin, the critic, the unbeliever. "It's isolated. It's making me sick. I see no smiling faces—except the singer, and he gives a little smile."

Barefoot Stan Walker, twenty-one, at our table, who was "trying to find a place to live" and admitted "I have not found anything great in life," wasn't much help. Nor were Lori Campbell, sixteen, or Mavis Mearns, nineteen. Both had been fasting for Jesus in hope of a revival in Vancouver.

Then entered Carolyn Sim, quiet at first, unnoticed, beaming, with a story that came out eventually over the candles.

At sixteen she had run off to Detroit from her home town of St. Thomas, Ontario.

"Each week I told my mother I was going to a dance, but I didn't, and I saved my money."

Carolyn beamed, like a girl who had never even stolen icing from a cake pan.

She said that two years ago she had looked ghastly, trying to appear older than sixteen, when she took a bus for Detroit. She had on an Indian print dress then, her hair up, "a floppety hat, glasses, heels, nylons, a lot of make-up. I had no ID, and my knees were knocking." But she got through on the bus without being questioned.

Carolyn, the former cheerleader, met a girl friend in Detroit. "She knew two guys."

They were drug pushers, and Carolyn found she was soon having as much as "eight hits of acid a day."

"I had everything—acid, speed, hashish, MDA, THC, mescaline. I got really heavy. Dad came. I was really messed up."

She was given counseling, sometimes three hours a day. She took off for Toronto.

"I was panhandling in order to eat."

She moved in with a man. She was now on psilocybin, a hallucinogen.

"I was really out of it in a really bad space. I didn't care what my parents thought. They couldn't kill me."

An uncle intervened and talked her into going to Edmonton. She was already three months pregnant. She ended up in Calgary at the Bankview School for unwed mothers. She had her baby— ten months ago—whom she called Joselyn, but soon lost custody.

Next came a "fashion" kick. "I got sophisticated and I put everybody lower than me. Then I left everything. I was too messed up again, freaked out on MDA."

She hitchhiked to Vancouver.

The tale was not over. Robin, the cynic, was listening. "Wow," Robin couldn't believe so much happening to one so young and sweet—and saintly.

Carolyn told of being picked up by a Bible-carrying Frenchman. "I started to wonder what life is all about."

Carolyn moved into an acid commune in an abandoned ghost town fifty miles north of Parkhurst. "Most of the time," she said, "I was stoned. It was really a bad trip." At times she thought she had died.

She hitchhiked back to Vancouver. "I was just going to trip around, meeting people. One guy on the street talked about the love of Jesus. I accepted Jesus. I began the change the same day. Jesus was really real.

"For two years I had been searching for love and had not been satisfied. I was going the wrong way to get it together. Jesus cleaned up my life. He brought peace and joy I never knew before. And pure love. I don't need drugs any more."

Carolyn lives with other girls in the Jesus People Army's House of Rebekah in Vancouver. "I don't know how God works, but I am not afraid any more."

She looked as sweet by candlelight as if she was about to celebrate her first communion.

"Let the children come to me, do not hinder them; for to such belongs the kingdom of God." (Mk. 10:14).

"Wow," said Robin, who now had her own glow. "Wait till I tell my friends at work about her!"

II

There are saints, of course, among the young men and some of their leaders, but the saintliness seems to be largely among those in the front ranks rather than among the administrators, the elders. Not good saint material, the elders often have more on their minds than the practice of holiness as they "keep it all together."

The elder comes off a little harassed, as he calls the prayer meetings, raps and reads Scripture, and listens. Sometimes he's worrying about who has the kitchen duty for the next week since Jane and Harry split to go to a rural commune. Or he's worried not only about the absence of helpers in his house but about whether too many of the clan have been sent out too soon and too long on a mission outreach to try to save souls on some distant beach or in some distant state.

Saintliness rules cut most older types who have come circuitous routes. Although they have faith or at least the semblance of faith, most oldsters in the movement seem to have been impelled by other motives, consciously or unconsciously, in their move-in on the Jesus youth.

One of the three questions a researcher is most often asked about the Jesus People by those who are looking on from the side lines is: "Are they sincere?" (The other two most often asked questions are "Is it all a fad?" and "Where does the money come from?" The latter question will be discussed later in this book.) By and large I find the youths very sincere, but I grew to distrust immensely most of the big evangelists or prima donnas who are corralling the movement into networks and structures dependent on them. However, there are some exceptions.

You don't expect tradition-minded people, accustomed to a formal and what the newer generation would consider dull worship, to have much to do with saintliness, the saintliness of sacrifice, joy, God and a new countenance.

The Rev. Allen D. Hansen, fifty-four, a quiet man in turtleneck sweater, looked pretty square, with neither the zap nor zip for sainthood. But the Jesus People—the passion of his life now—are making him look like a saint along with the youngsters. Friends from the Salt Co., a three-story coffee-house ministry, of Hollywood Presbyterian Church, took me over to Pastor Hansen's Renewal House. They said I was passing through and needed a bed for the night. Unlike the huckster radio evangelists and other magnets, Pastor Hansen lives humbly with his kids in a seventeen-room house between central Los Angeles and Hollywood, funded by the intersynodical Lutheran Social Service of Southern California.

I arrived at this house, as I had at others, in old jeans from the Salvation Army, T-shirt, old paint sweater, tennis shoes—and a six-month massive straggly beard. Fortunately, looking ten to fifteen years younger than I am, without grey hair, I could get by. (I wore the sweater—or long hang-out shirt—to hide my one giveaway sign, my pudgy stomach.) I remember in Milwaukee, as a new guest in a Jesus People house, I had to check by phone with the elder who was away, a standard procedure. "How old are you?" he asked. "About twenty-seven," I said. He retorted: "What do you mean 'about'?"

At Renewal House I was braced for one of the usual questions, "Are you a Christian?" or "Are you saved?"

Neither question was asked. It was within a half hour of lights out time, so I was shown to a comfortable bed, one of five in a spacious upper room.

Next morning I was one of the first down to breakfast, where Mrs. Hansen, soul-faced, motherly, was busy in the kitchen, assisted by a mustached youth, Richard. A sign separated the hardboiled eggs from the soft-boiled eggs.

Pastor Hansen showed up in his turtleneck sweater, and he then called out through the house, "Breakfast time. We're going to eat whether you are up or not." Soon, almost from the woodwork, a dozen young men, a girl who lives in the former servant quarters of the mansion over the garage and two girl visitors from Salt Lake City, plus two other girl visitors who split after breakfast, were on hand. Most settled for oatmeal with honey. The young men at my table had smiles on their faces that covered pasts involving police records, foster homes and bad drug trips. One of them inquired if I were a Christian. Most were just busy trying to get awake.

Soon Mrs. Hansen turned around from an adjoining table and showed an interest in me. When she asked if I was hitchhiking, I'm sure my explanation that I was just drifting through, maybe going back to Detroit, "moving along," didn't really satisfy her. But this dedicated, loving woman had long ago learned not to ask too many questions.

Somehow the spirit of love was very strong. It came out in a relaxed but very heartwarming way in the Bible study.

One of the boys had written a song, and they sang it first, with guitar. "Don't let the devil get you down, boys; when he starts messing up your mind, boys, just call on the name of Jesus; don't let the devil get you down."

They talked of the Ten Commandments. The bearded, straggly, spiritual-eyed young men did not warm up to the rapping about not worshiping images or the meaning of the day of rest. But when the talk turned to parents, their hearts broke open.

You felt as if you were sitting within their hearts, hearing something more personal than a confessional, as Pastor Hansen guided them.

"If I were to analyze your relationships to your parents," said Pastor Hansen, "I would say it would be zero, for 90 per cent of you, but I am not blaming anyone."

Said one: "I wouldn't say I hate my father, but the way he treated me. . . ."

Pastor Hansen talked of Christian responsibility—regardless of past estrangements—such as letting parents know where you are, writing them. . . .

Another said: "We are copies of our parents, even though we may hate them. If you hate your parents, you cannot be at peace with yourself; you hate yourself."

Carleton from Columbus, Georgia, began to open his heart: "I got some of Daddy's habits." He went on to describe how his dad swore at him and said he was unwanted and made unkind comments about his mother. "Only time my father ever talked to me was when he was bombed. He would 'ah,' and 'uh,' and 'uh,' and I would say to him, 'Can't you talk English?' "

Pastor Hansen went on to point out how in history some people who were total wipeouts became totally soft hearted. "Look at lousy Saul, the hater. He is the one who wrote a chapter on love. God turned the sourpuss into a radiant person. God can take your background—and the Bible is full of him doing so—and turn it into an opportunity."

Pastor Hansen told of visiting a fellow who had stopped in the house for one day and who was now in jail serving a sentence of six months to ten years. He read a letter penned by that youth: "I couldn't believe the change that came over me after being at the House of Renewal. At first I was kind of discouraged. . . . I had really prayed for the power of the Holy Spirit. But I didn't feel anything. My parents came to get me. But by the time I got home, I felt a change. I smiled, and it was on my face all day long. The Holy Spirit grin. I still have it. My body is at peace with God. Worldly desires are gone, like you said, and you were right, I don't miss them. It's beautiful how the Holy Spirit stepped in."

Pastor Hansen, when asked, said the youth had been convicted of killing a woman while driving under the influence of drugs. "I hope to go back at six months and get him committed to us . . . and do everything I can . . . and he lost his girl friend, too, and you know, he is radiant. He is beginning prison with a smiling face, can you imagine?"

Pastor Hansen concluded on the commandment to love parents. "The greatest honor to a parent is what you can become. The greatest dishonor is to cop out."

In the prayer session that followed, while others hesitated, Carleton prayed four different times. First: "Thank you for a good Bible study. I hope everybody is touched as deeply as I. Oh, Jesus, touch my father. As far as I know, he is still an alcoholic. I heard him say many times he will go crazy before he dies. Oh, Jesus, show him your way as you showed me, and make a new man out of him."

Another: "Lord, help that guy in prison. . . ."

Carleton again: "Thank you, thank you, Jesus. . . ."

Herman: "Help my father and stepfather and uncle so they will not do cruel things any more. . . ."

Pastor: "Thank you for the privilege of being your children. Thank you for your love despite everything. Make us over so we love you."

They held hands and sang.

I left, a visitor in disguise, with a good feeling in my heart about Renewal House.

And later, when I thought about saints, I thought of Pastor Hansen's quiet, unheralded, loving but effective work.

III

Saints in Jesus' eyes were never the haughty, the rich, the ego trippers. He identified with the "least" (Matt. 25:45). And the saints of history were the simplest. Observes Kieran Quinn: "I saw in the soiled face of the child of God (still kneeling in the moist earth, oblivious to the rock cacophony) the visage of that Jesus Freak from centuries ago, a man who shocked his contemporaries by his compelling, simple gospel life—Francis from the small town of Assisi." [1]

The Jesus People movement, with its more than 800 communes, is a great leveler. There are many who are the least in a Jesus house. Yet, as in many families, there are also the favorites (a point that can break up communes as well as families, Andrew Greeley points out). With the Jesus People, sometimes the least—the ones who seem almost to be forgotten or overlooked in their own ranks—can appear to be the saints, the Cinderellas, the hidden princes, likely destined for the golden streets in the final reckoning.

It is six A.M. in the House of Joy, one of the half dozen satellite communes related to the Maranatha Assemblies of God Church on the northeast side of Portland.

The House of Joy is just that.

In some communes, the young people get up when they please, sometimes traipsing around in bathrobes until noon, but not in the House of Joy.

"Hallelu, hallelu, hallelu. . . ." Like a bird tripping through the tree tops, slim, angelic-faced Troy goes up and down the corridors of the House of Joy, never waking anybody up immediately —just singing.

At first, from a sleeping bag in a corner of the attic in the overcrowded all-male monastic type of house, you hear Troy's high-throated "hallelu's." They grow louder, and then go down again. Like a bird fluttering through the house. Like the gentle breeze of the Spirit of God, thankful for a new day, anxious to live it.

He pokes his head in at the door at last and asks your name. "Praise God."

Troy is soon heard down in the kitchen, from which he later (after a long but also joyful prayer service of the men in the house, at least one of them an all-American athlete) serves forth a vat of Ralston and another of oatmeal, with all kinds of trimmings available—honey, cracked soy beans, nuts, dried fruit, preserves and milk.

When the prayer meeting starts in the living room, Troy breezes in and out from his cooking duties and stops short in the dining room by the long monastic table, made of beautiful old planks from a chicken coop, covered and nurtured over with resin polish.

It is Troy who sets the pace for the hand-waving spiritual free-for-all of barefoot men in undershirts and sport shirts in prayer before breakfast.

"Hallelu, hallelu . . . Jesus, thank you, Lord . . . Hallelujah," Troy sings.

"Blessed be the name of the Lord . . . holy, holy, holy. . . ."

Troy is on his knees, his face turned up in prayer.

If ever a man looked, acted and sounded like a saint. . . .

IV

Then there is the special, unexpected, less dramatic kind of saint who must surely be after Jesus' own heart. I am sure the leaders of the well-oiled Jesus People Army, with all of its holdings and houses in the Pacific Northwest and British Columbia, pay little attention to Jerry Mandeville, twenty-one.

He is one of the many Canadian youths who hear tales of the Pacific Coast—its beauty, its liveliness, its many freaks—and who drift out west from the East. Jerry came out from Montreal, got in with the Jesus People, got his mind messed up again and was asked to leave. He joined them on a farm again, but the steady Bible rapping wore him down. He seems to be more at ease just hanging on at the side lines. He works at car washes when he can get work and lives in a free room in a flophouse, where the manager took pity on him. His room is next to that of a handsome young lad who also drifted west from Montreal and who shines shoes for a living.

Jerry took pity on me one night at one A.M. in Vancouver, when all the Jesus houses were full. He tried to get me into one of the houses split off from the Jesus People Army headquarters, waking everybody up and explaining things in French. But that house had long been put to rest. So Jerry took me back to his own little flop-house, gave me his room and settled himself on the floor in his buddy's room. The next day we rapped a good bit as he took me around to other Jesus spots and I gave him a ride down to Seattle. Never an unkind word about Jesus People leaders whom some of his associates criticized, and he made a point of buying us both ice cream cones out of his limited funds as I was checking out a Jesus People center upon arriving in Seattle. A quiet happiness. Jerry looked out for others, giving up his own comfort without a thought about it. Unheralded. A saint whom others would over-look. A saint, nevertheless.

V

The purpose of introducing you to some of the saintly types in the heart of and at the edge of the movement—which also has its sinners—is to help set the theme of this book, which strives to deal with the central, most often asked question, "Is the movement a fad?" and the correlative, "Where is it going?" It is not likely to be simply a fad, if for no other reason than the growing organization of the movement by outsiders. But, more basic still, you find when you are suddenly faced with saints that it would be hard to brush off the whole thing as a fad, even if there were no outside organizers.

If the people themselves demonstrate a deep inner peace and other qualities more profound than can be accounted for by scientific explanations, that depth of dedication also hints of some perpetuity. It must be remembered, too, that the personal com-mitment of the Jesus People is not peculiar to them, but, as Theo-dore Roszak and R. D. Laing point out, the personal style is a distinguishing factor of the whole counterculture. Saintliness, at least in some of its aspects, is not limited to the Jesus People. There is a general kind of sainthood that has roots in the counter-culture and where it is going, and not in hermit sands.

What does all this new saintliness—personal commitment, dedi-cation, the power of changed lives—mean?

We have not delved into the *why*'s of the movement, such as discussing if the youths are acting out of father or hero complexes, out of a sense of isolation, authoritarian hunger, the anxieties of post-adolescence, the influence of materialism and technocracy, the purposelessness of life, the effects on the young of fluctuations in the economy and wars, abnormal psychology patterns or the various church styles that bore and turn off youth.

The purpose of this book is to take the discussion onto a much needed new stage, permitting the Jesus People movement to interpret itself in such areas as race, sex, theology, structure, the effect on culture and the future. Some speculation—a synthesis of all the extensive variety of input—is needed. But there are more pressing questions than the much reported "why" that need exploration now that the movement is here. What has the Jesus People movement to contribute:

For culture?

For the church?

For society at large? Where is the Jesus People movement going?

2

Where Are the New Saints Marching To?

Take note of this scene: Young people are sitting around on the floor of a private home. They sing the old hymns, read Bible passages, and give their testimonies. They come largely from one of the area high schools. Faces aglow, they talk of prophecy, the Bible as their sole rule of life, and their passion for winning their fellow students to Jesus.

Praise God!

But now, let me add, this is *not* a Jesus People scene. This is a scene at a Hi-C meeting of more than twenty years ago when I was in high school.

Watching the Jesus People today—of high-school and just past high-school age—for the most part sitting around on the floor studying their Bibles and singing, I ask: Is there any difference from the youthful Bible studies in the homes and in the school cafeterias of a past generation? Another has in effect answered that question. "I like to say that I've been in the Jesus movement for twenty years," said William R. "Bill" Bright, founder and president of Campus Crusade for Christ, International. Begun in 1951, that organization now has a staff of 3,000 ministering to students and dropouts and military personnel.[1]

Indeed, a Jesus People rally I witnessed in November, 1971, in Worcester, Massachusetts, billed as an all-New England Jesus

People rally, was so churchy and so much like old Youth for Christ rallies that it really made me wonder if the movement is over and the church is swallowing it up. But just as the radicals are not the whole movement nor the moderates the whole movement, neither are those who sponsor and attend churchly types of rallies, even though they are growing in numbers. But, my, how much like church! You could even point at the men on the platform and say which ones were paid directors of religious education or executives of organized church ministries, identifying them by their formal, smooth and polished—if not artificial—smiles and correct language.

The audience in the Little Theatre, Worcester, was a mixture of freak types, Sunday-school twelve-year-olds and parents. They tried, though, with a canned "Give me a J-e-s-u-s, what do we do with it, go, go, go" cheer, a syncopated "I got peace of mind," some "Oh, wow" disjointed, uncompleted testimonies of teens who blinked their eyes sweetly as the parents smiled. There was a glee club from a nearby Bible school and one jump-up-and-down song, like the old "Fishers of Men."

In areas where the Catholic charismatic movement has influence, some Jesus People gatherings also look much like old-time church, but with a little more chanting and quiet control. Thus at Central Northwest Presbyterian Church, Detroit, on a Friday night, Leo Sabatini, from the Word of God Community (Catholic Pentecostal), Ann Arbor, bearded and in T-shirt and corduroys, led in the singing of mimeographed songs, paced Bible readings, and put announcements here and there.

At first glance, therefore, the Jesus People movement looks like a rerun of an old movie. Indeed, scholars see parallels all the way back to the start of Christianity. The disciples roamed the streets, met by the riverside, baptized in the rivers, saw visions, shouted with joy, wrote their own hymns, met in cellars and convened on week nights as they broke away from a one-day establishment type of religion.

I

You can compare the Jesus People to the Gnostics of the first three centuries of the Christian church, particularly if you listen to them expatiate on the presence of heavenly bodies, angels and demons. Gnostics ranked emanations, revealed levels of God and illumination, on the one hand, and the array of lesser and evil lights on the other. Nathan Adler, the sociologist, is one of those who makes this comparison,[2] noting that gnosticism originated at a time when barbarians were crossing the frontiers, inflation was widespread and many feared the end of the world. The Gnostics rose with their emphasis on meditation and feelings over against reason and logic, as they rejected the established church and civil authority. Adler argues that as society becomes reordered and satisfies popular needs, such groups disappear.

Priest-columnist I. J. Mikulski notes of the Jesus People, "Their disdain for material possessions is in the finest Christian tradition of the early mendicant (begging) orders. Their simplicity of life, dependence on the Providence of God and the sincerity of their prayer life are all admirable qualities." [3]

Their style is distinctly monastic. They live on handouts or what the head of the order—an adult evangelist or pastor or radio preacher, such as an abbot, or the local elder (prior)—decrees. They pray and study at prescribed times of day and perform ordered tasks. Like the mendicants—Augustinians, Dominicans, Franciscans and Carmelites—they insist that God will provide. And money is found under a glass or in an envelope in the mail, or some bill is mysteriously paid, most often by a sympathetic layman who has heard them speak in his church or by somebody with a mission zeal, or even by youngsters in that particular commune.

Dr. Eugene Bianchi, of Emory University, Atlanta, tells me he sees in the movement the enthusiasm and dedication of the novitiate in Roman Catholic orders. He sees strength in their sense of commitment, but Bianchi, who has left the Jesuit order, believes the Jesus People, like their Catholic traditional monastic counterparts, will "have to cope with the problems of the scientific world."

"They remind me of, in church history, the emphasis on mysticism and the pietistic movements," said the Rev. James A. Lokken, an American Lutheran and a co-editor of the Liturgical Conference, Washington. "I tend to expect from this group problems that were in those earlier groups." He cited a revival in Norway 150 years ago when the emotional protestors ended up with the same rigidity they had protested.

To Dr. Edward P. Blair, retired professor of New Testament at Garrett Theological Seminary, Evanston, Pietism is a recurring phenomenon, running its course and dying before re-emerging. "The 'back to Jesus' emphasis recurs in Christian history," he says. "It is to be seen especially in pietistic movements of Protestantism. It represents a swing of the pendulum away from ecclesiastical and social emphasis in Christianity."

In the seventeenth century, Philipp Jakob Spener sparked a Pietist reaction against the rigidity of the state church that expressed itself in terms remarkably like those used by modern Jesus youth. Spener began developing a "warmer Christian life" with home Bible studies, which he called *collegia pietatis* (thus Pietism). He suggested a way of reform against immorality, laxity on the part of the laity and indifference within the church by a program of Bible reading and preaching for building up the soul, as contrasted to arguing over issues. He rejected the theater, cards, dancing. His movement—a seventeenth century Jesus movement— caught on at the University of Leipzig in 1686, and here a group (*collegium philobiblicum*) was founded for the study of the Bible. The Pietists developed a passion for evangelizing and launching missions.

With the Moravians, an outgrowth of Pietism in the seventeen hundreds, Christians began to travel about wherever the spirit led to seek souls for the Lord. Nicolaus Ludwig von Zinzendorf allowed exiles from Bohemia and Moravia to settle on his estate near Dresden. The group called their settlement Herrnhut and chose elders as leaders in 1727. The group became pious and almost monastic with its daily routine of prayers and the separation of men and women. Zinzendorf had no intention of taking the group out of Lutheranism. But as historian Williston Walker notes, "The separatist tendencies slowly won the upper hand . . ." [4] and "in spite of Zinzendorf's dislike of separatism, Moravianism was becoming more fully a church. In 1742 it was so recognized in Prussia by the Government. By 1745 the Moravian Church was thoroughly organized with bishops, elders, and deacons." [5]

The Methodists at their inception followed a kind of Jesus

People script. Charles Wesley and two friends at the University of Oxford launched a little club of their own in connection with their school studies, but soon gave much time to prayer and distributed communion. Joined by John Wesley, they were soon mocked as the "holy club" by fellow students, and one gave them the name of "Methodists," because they were so methodical. "They were very far as yet from what Methodism was to be. They were still a company painfully bent on working out the salvation of their own souls." [6] As Bianchi describes how some of the Jesus People at Emory are willing to be laughed at by their peers, you think of the Methodists, who although they did not entertain any thought of breaking with Anglicanism, nevertheless became one of the largest worldwide Protestant groups, with its own brand of formalism. "As in John Wesley's day, these [Jesus] people are searching for a reality apart from the church because the church has somehow failed to minister to them." [7]

A further similarity with the Wesleys—and later revivalists—is the preoccupation of the Jesus People with new music. Rarely do you hear any of the old-time hymns. They write their own. Notes John R. Sampey III, of Louisville, responding to the Southern Baptist *Home Missions* issue about the Jesus People:

Music with a new freedom, relevance and dimension has played a vital part in the great revivals of the past. Martin Luther both wrote hymns and largely started congregational singing. John Wesley preached while Charles Wesley touched the soul with . . . spiritual music. Moody had Sankey and the great hymn, "The Ninety and Nine". . . . Billy Sunday had Rodeheaver and Billy Graham has Beverly Shea. . . . The phenomenon of music turning on the soul to God is hardly new. We need not be too concerned about the emotionalism in the Jesus Movement. It was in evidence particularly in the Wesley and Finney revivals, yet positive long-range results testified these spiritual awakenings were not of men.[8]

Applying the experience of the Wesleyan revival directly to the present day is difficult because modern technology, with the sudden exposure provided by the electronic mass media, offers only a short space of time in which to try out a new idea and gives but a short life expectancy to any new idea. "Concerning history," said Dr. Martin Marty, professor of modern church history at the University of Chicago, "I've learned that the biggest liability is to be born in our century. In the past you could hide in the mountains for a century or two and make an impact. Now everyone exposes everything, and you can't get it together." Wesley was a rare talent who had "experience plus," says Marty. "The current crowd has experience but not organization, at least not yet." Says Dr. Henlee H. Barnette, professor of Christian Ethics, Louisville, Ky., "The Wesleys' 'Holy Club' was more sophisticated and socially concerned. This the Jesus People must possess if they are to make any significant impact on society."

The Salvation Army began like the Methodists, with perhaps more street orientation than the Methodists at the outset. William Booth, a Methodist, took to the streets, but in the course of sixteen years developed a formal, tightly organized movement with rank and discipline and a structured system of beliefs. In the United States, the Disciples of Christ grew out of efforts of Thomas Campbell, a Presbyterian, who moved to an open concept of the church, allowing communion for all, accepting no creed except the Bible and emphasizing the need of all men to accept Christ as savior. Like his European counterparts, Campbell had no intention of founding a church, but with time it ended up that way. Pietism, which begins as unstructured protest, seems destined to end up with its own formalism and institutionalism.

II

Where the Jesus movement is going, of course, nobody knows. And futurologists such as Herman Kahn, Anthony Wiener and Peter Drucker are quick to point out that unpredictables in any future and the element of "discontinuity" (Drucker's term) prohibit drawing direct parallels. Pat Boone declares that everything is up for grabs as it was in the first century. "I say the Jesus movement is Jesus moving," Boone told me in an interview in his living room in Beverly Hills. "Jesus is moving in the first century manner. He is really moving in this fantastic ground swell which is reaching out." Boone, disfellowshipped from his church for speaking in tongues, conducts his own services for his family in his home and baptizes Jesus People in his pool. "The greatest movement in the church is back to the home," he says. "House to house" as in the first century. He expects Christ may come in a few years and does not look for the emergence of any great structures in the meantime. "All of nature is groaning, grinding to a halt, for a new creation."

This sense of the urgency of the last days is shared by many Jesus People, but even so, they normally do not seem obsessed like older evangelists with theories and details of the Second Coming. Assessing the future in terms of Jesus' return, Ken Doty and Jeff Swindenman of Christian House, Athens, Ohio, say: "We expect to see much persecution even by the mid-1970's. We can only hope for Christ to return."

"Who knows, we may not be here that long," says Joel Kischel, director of the Cleveland, Ohio, Jesus Center.

Some of the Jesus People leaders see a coming evolvement of the movement, and not necessarily obliteration by the imminent Second Coming. Suppose it were 1980—what would the Jesus movement be like then, I asked some of the Jesus People. "It will be much larger," says Paula Brody, deaconess of the Hosanna House, Eugene, Oregon. "It will have more communal houses, especially back East, and more New Testament churches. Just more people praising the Lord!" Says Paul Campbell, elder of the fifteen-member Twenty-Third Psalm House, Nashville, Tennessee, "Jesus People will join with people in the churches who really want to follow God. Houses will give way to communities of Christians living in a certain area—working, then coming together to fellowship." An elder of His House, Indianapolis, Indiana, says that the movement "will probably work into the organized religions to revitalize them or set up independent churches." From Springfield, Illinois, Tom Richardson, director of the Lighter Side of Darkness House, says, "Guessing, I would think the extreme zeal now prevalent would have subsided quite a bit as the movement would have touched most everyone, with those that have been saved living and continuing to develop in their Christian lives. Also by then I believe we can expect strong opposition from those still deceived by Satan." John M. Kachelmyer, director of Christian Mission to Youth, Inc., of New Mexico, a former missionary to Japan now opening a "crash pad," House of Peace, in Albuquerque, says, "It will depend on whether or not the movement relies on the Spirit of God for leadership. If not, by 1980 it will probably be a semi-structured sort of thing, almost denominational like. There will be splits and factions. This need not be."

Wendell Woodthorp and Jim Talley, of the Church in the Park, Modesto, say: "If the leadership comes, it should move into the churches and we should have a national revival! If the revolution comes, it may be the only church left after the radicals burn the buildings!"

Miss Dorothy Savage, a program assistant of the National Council of Churches, says:

By 1980 there are many urban and rural communes. Some of them are organized around community celebration of transcendent experiences, and the rituals include happy, laughing, singing and spontaneous elements. Persons are accepted, be they emotional or silent. There are some "reformed" church buildings where the "ritual" services resemble these communal services. There is good attendance. There are many traditional services in many churches. Some elderly persons can be seen attending regularly. I would like to "dream" into 1990, where the Union of Jesus Communes has just held its annual general board meeting, and discussed the need for finding how to include under-twenty-one-year-olds who are no longer attending because of the prohibition on drug usage for enhancing religious experience . . . but then, 1980 is only nine years away!

George Aichele, Jr., a Garrett Theological Seminary student who helped run the Catacombs, a house for three married couples and a single person in Chicago, believes some person of charisma might take over a greatly diminished remnant of the Jesus People and give it some identity by 1980. Making it clear that he is not one of the Jesus People, Aichele says, "I suspect it [the movement] will be like Zen Buddhism or the Maharishi yoga or most other contemporary religious phenomena, a continuing presence, but also 'established' and much diminished in appeal."

"Since the movement is a part of the revolution of the times," observes Dr. J. Stillson Judah, professor of the history of religion at the Graduate Theological Union, Berkeley, California, "it will tend to disappear with the change of conditions, unless a charismatic leader were to come upon the scene to unite the separate groups and give it a strong organization, which it does not now have. In that case it could result in a new Christian sect. Without such leadership, the members will either return to their former beliefs or will join one of the evangelical or pentecostal sects."

Most scholars agree there will be an evolvement of the movement. Some share the view of Dr. Thomas Driver, of Union Theological Seminary, who in a speech at the Ecumenical Institute at Graymoor, New York, expressed the belief that the new youth culture signals a new historic era, a turning of the corner from the age of reason, from the age of logic and of analysis to the age of synthesis, itself a peg in an evolving process. And, as Miss Savage interprets that speech: "I believe this movement from 'reason' to be partly manifested in the present Jesus movement."

Few put it as precisely as Dr. John Cobb, of Claremont College, who says it will either develop into a new denomination or peter out. Dr. Robert Kysar, of Hamline University, St. Paul, Minnesota, says only, "It will no longer exist in any form which is continuous with the one we know." And the Rev. Dr. James McCord, president of Princeton Theological Seminary, says, "Some, by 1980, will have a deepened and more mature faith, while others will be disillusioned and will be following other fads." Such statements at least underscore the element of change that is in the wind for the movement.

"The tendency toward more formal and organized approaches will occur as some followers institutionalize their faith," says Dr. John Paul Eddy, associate professor of education, Loyola University of Chicago. "The trend of most of these types of movements is to peak and level off. Some of the followers will go into main-line denominational groups and change them even as they become like their members. Others may leave any religious community and become lone religious mystics or agnostics. Their perfectionalism for ideals will cause them to be disillusioned with religious group activities. Again, some will continue in smaller groups that exist today waiting for the resurrection of another revival!"

The Rev. Dr. Paul A. Crow, Jr., of Princeton, New Jersey, chief staff officer for the merger talks of nine denominations involving 26 million Protestants, told me that by 1980 the Jesus People "will still be a leavening influence on all of us, and they will help in calling the church back to basic things." He praised the Jesus People for "staying close to the normatives of faith, such as the Lordship of Jesus Christ and Scripture."

Hans Küng in his speeches and conversations also notes the positive direction of the Jesus People movement. The controversial but influential priest at Tübingen University in Germany says, "The Jesus People movement is a challenge to all in the church and to the progressive people especially, people who thought they were relevant just talking about church, and they are a challenge to theologians who never make a serious exegesis on Jesus. . . . Maybe Jesus was a little different . . . and certainly more human than the Jesus of our theological method. We cannot define the church without Jesus. A Christian is not just one of good intentions."

III

At the moment, the Jesus People are doing what Charles A. Reich says the new exponents of Consciousness III—the new style that has erupted beyond the traditional approach of Consciousness I and the technocracy of Consciousness II—must do. "Consciousness III must reach beyond youth or fail," [9] says Reich.

Recently I visited with a group of men who work on a diesel assembly line in Detroit, all middle-aged or older, as they met in a union hall for after-work worship and prayer. I asked their leader about the Jesus People. He said, "They're about the same as any other church group." Others among these close-cropped Middle America types told of taking their teens down to have fellowship with the Jesus People, whom they are learning to appreciate. To the extent that they are counterculture or a part of a new creative culture in which man shapes his own goals on nontechnical lines, the Jesus People are shaping a future for themselves and others. They are transcending some of the gaps. This may yet prove to be the unique contribution of religion, which needs no special talent or training as do the arts and other forms of cultural achievement.

Dr. Walter C. Hobbs, of the State University of New York,

Buffalo, notes that time and attrition themselves are formalizing forces. The mere act of continuing to exist generates formalizing and structuring forces. "My guess is," he says, "that the life-style preferences of the street people will increasingly influence those of the larger society, especially as the street people become the larger society, and the movement will institutionalize even to the point of general acceptance, though not necessarily widespread adoption."

This participation in a wider scene affecting society guarantees the Jesus People some future, particularly if the generational revolt is not likely to die down in a few years, as Roszak argues.[10] For the Jesus People are a part of this revolt, sharing such elements of the counterculture as alienation, personalism, and a revolutionary stance. Harvey Cox underscores this theme. Over coffee and doughnuts in Ann Arbor recently, I asked him if he were to look back from a vantage point of 1980 what he would expect to see concerning the Jesus People. Cox, professor of divinity at the Harvard Divinity School, said, "If you include the commune movement in general (and not only the communes of the Jesus movement), this is a beginning of an enormous cultural movement.

"It is a movement away from the institutions which they feel have cheated them—the churches, the families, schools. Communes relieve the tension of 'competing' and piling things up. I sense people need a community to belong to, which leads them to sharing in a commune."

Cox has been active in a miniature commune of his own, sharing his house with another family. "Communes need some kind of symbolic and mystical binding, and the religious is the most available to the people," he said. Thus, in his view, the Jesus movement is more than a fad. Rather it is a part of the restructuring of society.

The commune is a larger concept to Cox than a mere gathering of people. It reflects the trend toward upheaval of all institutions in the name of interpersonal relationships and a surging antimaterialism. Thus to him the family concept is also up for grabs. He points out that the nuclear family, existing in isolation, often on the move, is foreign to nearly all concepts of human relations in history. Much of the Old Testament, he reminds us, is centered on polygamy, and Jesus is little concerned about the tightness of a little isolated family. "Who is my mother, and who are my brothers?" Jesus asked, and he replied as he stretched out his hand toward his disciples, "Here are my mother and my brothers!" (Mt. 12:48, 49).

One thing I have noted among the Jesus People. While not all are ex-drug addicts, most have had some experience of alienation from their parents and the nuclear family. Out of this experience the Jesus movement, if it continues, may well contribute to the demise of the American nuclear family, despite a strong emphasis among Jesus People on fidelity and on the sanctity of marriage. They will complain about the particular family backgrounds that they have experienced (sometimes tragically), and they will defend the future structure of their potential families (some are, of course, already married, with children). Despite their righteousness and acceptance of traditional views of the family, Jesus People have a larger "family" in which a child may have many associates and many adult images. Deriving benefits that are spiritual as well as psychological, the sincere young Christian commune dweller is helping to reorder society.

"The Jesus People phenomenon is first a socio-cultural trend and then, only derivatively, a religious trend," says Rocco Caporale, associate professor of sociology and director of research for Pitzer College, Claremont, California. Caporale, chief theologian of the Society of Priests for a Free Ministry, a former Jesuit, says:

Deprived strata of society regularly channel their need energy in the direction of religion. The Jesus People are conspicuous for meaning deprivation; theirs is a genuine invention which brings together extremes formerly thought as unreconcilable. It still misses the essence of religious experience by locating it in socio-cultural forms and using it as a pawn for cultural expressions.

Lambert Dolphin, a young former physics professor who runs an influential commune in a hillside mansion at Palo Alto, California, has written and distributed a mimeographed treatise on Christian communes (or communals, as he calls them). He first of all justifies the theology of the Christian commune ("the concept of an extended family is implicit in the church as the Body of Christ"), and goes on to say:

Christian communal is also very valuable for those who have never been raised in any kind of a Christian home, for those who have been raised in legalistic or traditional homes or schools where there has been a lack of freedom, openness, and tolerance of dissent. The great central value of the Christian communal is that it permits men and women to know themselves more fully as persons reborn and recreated in the likeness of Jesus Christ. In a society where so much of family life is in need of healing, a great deal of new life and love is potentially available in the properly operating Christian communal, and the value of such groups in the society cannot be underestimated.

Throughout the history of the Christian Church, Christians have from time to time lived together in communals. There is always the danger of institutionalizing (a generation from now) that which today has life and vitality because of God's presence. It is important to stay loose and flexible in the communal, as elsewhere in the Church, and to pay very careful attention to the sovereign leading of God in all activities of the communal. It is only through diligence, constant study of the Scripture, through fervent and daily prayer, and through careful obedience to Jesus Christ that a communal can flourish. Life in the middle of a Christian communal can be very exciting, and it can provide a vital, wholesome, healing experience for those persons who need to discover more fully the humanity and love of Jesus Christ our Lord.

Already, the growth of communal concepts, either formal or informal (and quite apart from aberrations such as swingers' clubs, etc.) is affecting the structure of society, as apartments for singles and the elderly highlight communal facilities. I have just enrolled my daughter in Michigan State University and was amazed at the influence of the communal or community concept on dormitory life. She is in a big, self-contained center of students, with its own cafeteria, auditorium, lounges and library between the wings for men and women. Dr. Benjamin D. Zablocki, University of California sociologist, expects further communal influence on society as communes contract themselves out for businesses, certainly a trend among the Jesus communes (see Chapter 10).

Carl D. Onofrio, of the Dietrich Bonhoeffer (Lutheran) House near the University of Chicago (it is also the Lutheran Center) has done a study on *Communal Forms: Emergent Power Bases.* He rules out as empty and useless two institutions, the nuclear family and the Church. And on the premise that "destruction precedes construction, death precedes resurrection," he suggests a direction of new life through the communal concept. He discusses "historical" corrections to "institutional corruption and stagnation." Such corrections, he says, have included monasticism, the Puritan revolution, and the utopian, visionary communes of the nineteenth century. He discusses Brook Farm, near Boston; Oneida, in Upstate New York; New Harmony, in Indiana, and other forms. He says:

Puritan England represents a disciplined intentional attempt at reconstruction. An attempt that sought its gains largely through existing channels and was tenaciously prepared to see them through. Further, the notions of covenant and voluntary commitment, so key to the Puritans, will surely be a part of any communal movement.

The history of the utopian socialists must be culled for its many seminal ideas (i.e., small social units as the basis for reconstruction; the full cooperative, attractive, meaningful work). Some of the ideas were sufficiently prophetic to be of real use today. . . .

The communal experimentation of the 19th century America enriched our society in countless, and unforeseen ways. This fact should be sufficient warning against any outright condemnation of communal "dropouts." [11]

Onofrio discusses the Taize community in Chicago (offshoot from a small postwar Protestant monastery in a hillside sheep town in central France) and the Reba Mennonite community, with a history of fifteen years of successful sharing in Evanston. He cites the free church movement of Berkeley, California, which has carried on its radical demonstrations but has not proliferated successfully. I question the validity of his list of 2,000 "underground" churches, many of which involve little more than an extension of formal religion into a home while old memberships in existing church structures are continued. The house churches have been around for a long time. Their growth has been encouraged now by the celebration of home masses, but I doubt that they promise any really new directions except as they provide a matrix for new ideas.

IV

But the Jesus communes seem to be more a part of the new consciousness of which Roszak talks, with some perpetuity implied. Granted, Jesus houses are closing down all the time. Try and send a survey to them, and a large percentage of the letters will be returned because the commune left no forwarding address. But that does not negate their existence. A part of the Jesus People philosophy, like that of Zinzendorf and the Moravians, is to keep on the move and establish new colonies. People in the centers that remain open, on the other hand, can tell you the addresses of several other Jesus houses you never heard of.

The Jesus People are more than a fad and have a future because:

(1) They have money working for them, as outsiders bankroll their efforts and they themselves devise new ways of paying expenses. The money of evangelists and business tycoons can help keep the movement on the map, much as the Illinois Band, captained by Chicago real estate seller and produce dealer Benjamin F. Jacobs and others (including Philadelphia merchant John Wanamaker and H. J. Heinz, food tycoon), got the Sunday school movement off the ground in an earlier generation.[12]

(2) There is a wide diversity of individual religious experience that exists apart from the promoters. This experiential quality, shared with other communal and radical types, can become effective in social and political action (see Chapters 5 and 11), and guarantee the movement with its communes a future influence.

(3) The Jesus People generally consist of small groups and are more durable, much like a small family, in which even if only one person works there is some assurance of paying the rent.

(4) Although there are conflicts (see Chapter 4), there is little real heresy or deviation in the movement. Of course, this could be a negative factor, for many groups are created over conflicts, quarrel internally, and derive their energy in so doing. But again, the common ground of "Jesus only," communal styles and life in the Spirit aspects of the movement might hint at the emergence already of incipient denominations. Indeed, the process has developed to the point where some consolidation among structured groups, as we will see, is also at hand (Chapter 4). There

are still heretics in the movement. Some could cite the cult groups, of which the Children of God are the biggest and most popular, that refuse cooperation with society and with most other Jesus People. But the Children of God are not the whole picture, despite their noise, their prominence on TV documentaries and their new acquisitions. Historically, they will probably come out as an influential heresy that in time waned—or contracted—into a new denomination. Heretically, there is also the evasive Manifest Sons who, taking a Scripture reference (Rom. 8:19), believe themselves to be divine supermen. They had a house across from Shiloh House in Portland but have closed shop, and nobody knows where they are now.

(5) Most Jesus People make no demand on the individual in terms of political activism, nor does the movement demand much of society at the present (potentially, yes); the movement thus finds itself in a very favorable climate, acceptable to society (a condition that favors institutionalization if not the health of the movement).

(6) The Jesus People nevertheless remain a part of a continuing alienation—*i.e.*, alienation from family and church establishments (denominations)—which makes it difficult for them even to want to return to former milieus and structures.

(7) They are more nomadic than their fellow freaks. The network of published addresses of Jesus communes and a common cause encourage travel and visitation. The bus freaks on the secular side are settling down. I remember rapping with mystic-drug-orientated Stephen Gaskin in his bus on an early Sunday morning on the seashore in California. He and his multiple family have now settled on a farm in Tennessee. But the Jesus People are getting into the bus business. There's Steven Rafelsky's Symphony of Souls in Christ, headquartered in New York City, but now known as the Bus People as they traipse around the United States and Canada. The Pontiac, Michigan, House of Prayer has sent out several vans of youths—one freelancing around the country; one settling in Topeka, Kansas; another, a Joel's Army group, visiting Indian reservations in Arizona and California; another starting a coffee house with Northwestern Bible College students in Minneapolis, etc. Their youthful zeal is encouraged by the network but

also by the commission of Christ to be missionaries (Mt. 28:19, 20).

X (8) The Jesus People become bi- and tri-cultural. Turned off to society, they nevertheless begin to look fairly straight. Girls groom their hair immaculately, boys shave, etc. They speak and witness in straight churches. They stand with a foot in each consciousness— traditional, technical and the new, creative trying-to-emerge Consciousness III. Middle-class and generally sophisticated, many having attended college, they remain individuals, particularly as they relate to the smaller communes. Although appearing to be in a no-man's-land and potentially victims of the regular or counter-culture and various consciousnesses, they are still individuals, despite the fad of uniformity. They are not yet pawns in a cultural dialectic. Their voices are heard. They have options— going home to Mother, visiting a friend in another commune or seeking out places of leadership in some corner of the movement. The Jesus People have so proliferated that the death of one Brook Farm or Oneida Community or New Harmony or Koinonia or Walden II isn't going to faze them. In their flexibility, the Jesus People have considerable strength. They do have a potential for influencing society and for continuing and evolving into a new role or structure. And of course, history—if that means anything—is on their side.

As the Rev. Lloyd W. Putnam, educational director of the University of Michigan Office of Religious Affairs and former assistant dean of the University of Chicago Divinity School, puts it:

Movements do not develop in a vacuum and thus one can discern historically a judgment in the Jesus People upon a sterile theology, an irrelevant religious institutionalism, and a meaningless cultural situation. People desperately need some symbolic structure of meaning, and the Jesus People movement—with all its varied life-styles—indicates one response to that fundamental need.

Religious institutions are born and die—but do not totally disappear. The movement may become frozen in its own institutionalization and encapsulation. Time will tell. As of now, the movement clearly represents a judgment on the church and potentially the promise of new life for otherwise culturized main-line churches (if they will only listen and hear). With all of their dangers (anti-intellectual, romantic, simplistic, naivete about human nature, loss of tension between Gospel and Law, escape from freedom to new authority, etc.), the Jesus People yet present a freshness and vitality that might just become a viable part of the church of tomorrow.

3

Laboratory for
New Leaders

Once upon a time, there were no Jesus People, American Western style or Eastern or any style. There were entities such as Campus Crusade, Teen Challenge (the beat-the-drugs-with-the-Gospel clinics of Dave Wilkerson, of *The Cross and the Switchblade* fame), the work of a Southern California suburban pastor, a few evangelists watching the times, and a would-be entertainer trying to run a night club in the pious fundamentalist and pentecostal town of Springfield, Missouri, and later on educational TV in the Los Angeles area. The Spirit of God moved upon the face of the men involved, and behold, there was a movement. Media and cameras moved in, bright lights shone, and it was daytime for the Jesus People.

I

Taking credit for the start of the movement, particularly for the Jesus houses, is the Rev. John A. McDonald, fifty, pastor of the Mill Valley First Baptist Church and chairman of Evangelicals Concerned, Inc., a newly-formed group of seventy-five staff members that advises new Jesus houses and evangelistic programs. He organized The House of Acts in suburban San Francisco in 1967. McDonald regularly housed four or five couples in his House of

Acts in Novato. However, the traffic through there of various youths soon brought it to public attention. It's closed now, but McDonald regards many of the other houses as "spin-offs."

X Before that, Christian communes in mid-century included the late Clarence Jordan's Koinonia Farm in Americus, Georgia, an interracial experiment of a Southern Baptist theologian, and the Reba House of the Mennonites in Chicago. I remember another Mennonite House of young people, whites, in the Maxwell Street black ghetto in Chicago. I visited them and wrote an article on them twelve years ago. It would sound much like a Jesus People article today. Churches also had summer communes of youth work forces.

Campus Crusade was finding it difficult to reach the turned-off counterculture youth and seemed happier with going after the usual fraternity types. Jack Sparks, now forty-two, a professor, on the other hand, felt the gospel should be directed toward radical militants as well, and—with the encouragement of several former associates of Campus Crusade in California, among them Ed Plowman, a San Francisco pastor-church journalist, now with *Christianity Today*—the Christian World Liberation Front was developed. Located on Channing Way near the University of California campus, in a suite of offices, the movement ground out posters and handouts, including their own underground newspaper *Right On!* They have been praised for their persistence in doing battle with the radicals, holding their own on Sproul Steps at the University of California when loud-speakers were set up to drown them out.

However, my own observance of them at Sproul Plaza on one occasion was less favorable. I was sick to see how hungry the young people were for spiritual direction and then to observe that the one-track, unimaginative CWLF minds were unable to cope with debate or dialogue. The freaks tried to talk to the CWLF Jesus People, but as one freak said, "They won't listen to you, geez!" and "All they can do is quote Scripture like a robot!" On that particular occasion, sitting on the steps were students from India, looking as freakish as the others, and there was a girl in long-topped overalls with a public works clean-up bag on her back. All giving the CWLF an ear, all turned off. Somebody with a genuine love for these freaks instead of an ego trip of his own might have reached them. The situation raised in my mind the picture we journalists see all the time—denominational and other religious officers grinding out press-release material like mad, seeing to it that it gets distributed, only to have it discarded immediately in a newspaper office, sometimes unopened. The CWLF is great for its money and volume of output, but its influence is probably no greater than that of the church Ditto machine.

When I dropped in at CWLF again a year later, in 1971, Sparks had moved the operation farther from the campus, isolated in an upper story above a restless black ghetto. Radio equipment and stacks of publications all indicated that the CWLF was still dittoing. A Jesus person from out of the state, John Kachelmyer, of Albuquerque, New Mexico, visited the CWLF in Berkeley and observed that it was "solid. A pretty good place. The elders were unfriendly, though, but the others were super good." Good or bad, the CWLF and other streamlined organizations are not really needed by the Jesus People movement, as the houses across the nation grind out their own newspapers and relate to kids in less intellectually demanding and more personal raps. Sparks is working now to get a Jesus People news service off the ground, but many papers seem to have their own contacts and sources, as clippings are sent to them by friends around the country in other houses.

There are showmen in the business, who near the outset saw the bright lights, the publicity and the dramatics, but few would credit them with the origins of the movement. People like Arthur Blessitt, of Hollywood; Tony and Sue Alamo, of Hollywood, now Saugus, California; Morris Cerullo, in San Diego; George Bogle, in Detroit—all big people with flash and style.

Linda Meissner of the Jesus People Army, Seattle, is considered one of the pioneers. Duane Pederson of the Hollywood *Free Paper* and organizer of Jesus Festivals, is right at the hub of the movement. He declares in his book, *Jesus People:*

As far as I am able to determine, it began as the Holy Spirit began to work through a gal named Linda Meissner in the Seattle area. . . . Then from Seattle and the entire state of Washington, it seemed to leap down to the Southern California cities. In fact, at about the same time that

Linda began some work in Seattle, Chuck Smith's church opened its arms to the longhairs in Costa Mesa.[1]

Smith's church, Calvary Chapel in Orange County, near Costa Mesa and Santa Ana spreads along a side road among new upper-middle-class housing developments a mile from the San Diego expressway and an hour-plus drive out of Los Angeles, in the heart of conservative country. When Pederson describes Smith's interest in his freaks as "quite revolutionary," it is probably an understatement. The regular church members did by and large split when Smith opened the doors of his church, as the freaks came in and etched pews with the rivets on their levis, etc. About Calvary Chapel's communes he writes:

It started with just an apartment or Christian commune. I asked Chuck how it came about.

"Well, Lonnie Frisbee and some of these kids had no place to go. It seemed the Scriptural thing to do was to provide them with food and a place to sleep while we talked to them about the love of Jesus Christ.

"So we rented an apartment—on faith. We didn't have a lot of money. And before we knew it, we had 20 homeless street people living there. It was like wall-to-wall people. They could hardly breathe."

Chuck then rented a house. Within days it was crowded out. So, one at a time, they began opening up other communal Christian houses. And, one by one they filled up.[2]

Calvary Chapel now has eight communes. I picked one of them at random after a Calvary Chapel (standing room only) service on a Friday night. Mansion Messiah is an attractive lodge-like house sitting back from a strip of small industries, with ample parking in empty lots. You feel as if you are entering a real swinging party as handsome young men and chicks and freaks stand around socializing, eating, drinking. They are eating Jell-O and drinking pop and tea. The kitchen scene is like a Southern Baptist church basement pot luck supper. Jesus People from other houses who drop in bring food with them. The big social event is for the young people—usually after a church service—to go over to one of the other houses for a potluck. They alternate their visits to the various houses. Friday is Mansion Messiah's night. They break up before midnight, and the parking-lot scene of youths, tooling up or packing a wagon, is like that of any high-school Friday night recreation hour in a small town.

II

Up in the Northwest, Linda Meissner acknowledges that God did "reach out" and that "we were one of the first ones" in the Jesus People movement. But she adds that a group of youths meeting at Huntington Beach, California, south of Los Angeles, earlier had moved on to become a part of the Texas-based Children of God group with which she is now linked.

Raised on an Iowa farm, Linda came to New York in 1961 to help with Dave Wilkerson's work among the street gangs. In his book, *The Cross and the Switchblade,* Wilkerson said: "In one of her letters home, Linda wrote that her life was in constant danger. This was not an exaggeration." [3] He devotes a whole chapter to his pretty new assistant from the farm and her courage. She eventually took up the lecture trail and ended up in Seattle, where she decided to launch her own anti-drug program, which she called Youth Speak, Inc. Her projects include a grocery store used as an office for the Jesus People Army newspaper, *The Truth;* a girls' house, House of Esther; a counseling center, the Ark, a former storefront; a former Danish fraternal building that houses a men's house; a coffee house, the Catacombs; a gym; JPA offices; etc. Seattle newspaper reports tell how she can hold a youth audience spellbound for two and a half hours. A direct off-the-collar, honest type, "Oh yeah," she'll say often in an interview. This five-foot two-inch, light brown haired wife of a Seattle fireman has a knack for making friends, and despite a dramatic style seems to have generated no enemies or real critics, at least until she joined the Children of God.

She talks of her work as the army, the Jesus People Army, and the workers as soldiers, but she makes it clear that Christ is the supreme commander and she is just a field general. To her the Jesus People are revolutionaries, and their "unity of purpose and technique" promise, she says, a "spiritual revolution such as this nation has never seen before." [4] She even talks like a general. She told me: "We go in with an army and hit a city." They establish a beachhead, "and some people might stay on." The attack on sinners even has a military look at times. Once during a massive outdoor rock festival, she chartered a small plane and bombarded the crowd with 10,000 copies of her paper, as her "commandos" moved in among the crowd, and according to one report, "had a field day of witnessing." [5]

Duane Pederson may not be so important as his monopoly on national distribution of his Hollywood *Free Paper,* claiming up to 400,000 circulation, would seem to indicate. (Pederson does have his critics. One of them, John Kachelmyer, of the House of Peace, Albuquerque, calls the Hollywood *Free Paper* an "empty publication, mostly visual impact," and Kachelmyer prefers several other papers, such as *Icthus* in Boulder.) Yet as a coordinator and a hub nationally, if not locally, of the movement, Pederson is a man to reckon with. He has done much to give the movement a special strength by coordinating it through his newspaper. Each issue has an up-to-date (more or less) list of hundreds of Jesus houses, centers, and coffee houses, new and old. Thus, as we have noted, it encourages the mobility of the Jesus People, as they look up houses to visit in other communities, often near friends, and end up by staying. He is also responsible for introducing commercialism into the movement, by producing his own bumper stickers, etc., and carrying ads of new Jesus records and other products. You might say he is Americanizing, or westernizing, the cop-out Christians, making them quantitatively conscious again, preparing them for a role of some sort within society.

Pederson, aged thirty-three, probably looks as much like Billy Graham as anybody in the country. The similarity does not stop with just the handsome Nordic features, straight nose, keen, almost birdlike eyes, broad forehead and straight blond-brown hair. Both are national evangelists and close to a more *status quo* wing of evangelism.

Pederson has registered the name Jesus People with the United States copyright office, and gets very uptight when you talk about others using the name Jesus People on watches, as the Melodyland pentecostal-oriented center at Anaheim, California, is doing.

The six-foot two-inch Minnesota farm boy, in fairly new working jeans and matching jacket, finds himself on the quiet end of the spectrum of a movement that tends to take a fancy to speaking in tongues and shouting out songs.

Pederson, a sort of pope or archbishop without a parish, gets out and baptizes in the ocean, but he sees the kids going to various communes and centers. He is content to leave it that way. Like Graham, who also prefers to conduct rallies, Pederson likes to work with and speak encouraging words about the church. However, Pederson differs with Billy Graham about the future of the church. Graham has told Pederson and this writer that the future of the church is likely to be in small groups, as it was in the first century.

Pederson, although he says that the "churches will have to get with it or fold up," takes the unusual position (contrary to both many liberal leaders pushing unity and to conservative Jesus People turned off to main-line denominations) that the churches will come around and be strengthened by getting with the Jesus People types. "I see churches opening arms to all kinds of people now, as Christ did, which must be done again," he said, "and something is happening." He cited cases of big Baptist and Presbyterian churches, and independent churches, mushrooming with sudden new life as they seek to bring in the Jesus People and other youths with less formal approaches. And not just the conservatives. The big denominations, too. "I've got letters on my desk from the Lutheran Church in America and the American Lutheran Church and others asking help," he said.

"They all want to be where it is happening and not left out. I feel very optimistic. As people get turned onto Jesus Christ, they will get involved." Explaining how institutions can change, he cited the Roman Catholic church "which a few years ago began to get to basic principles and discard archaic principles."

Like modern ecumenists who worry about the division of denominations, Pederson worries about the divisions among the Jesus People, including such groups as the cultic Christian Foundation, a booming rural venture that started on the Sunset Strip. Its members were allegedly hassled by police, much as police constantly hassle, or search, tourists and hippies alike on the main streets of Hollywood and in the more freakish sections of Los

Angeles, such as the long coastal community of Venice that teems with freaks in the day and becomes a near ghost town at night. The Christian Foundation, with 300 members, and the cultic Children of God, now numbering several thousand, for the most part look on Pederson's efforts to work with the main-line churches and others of differing views as the work of the Devil.

When Pederson prays in his prayer meetings, the burden of his heart is clear: "Remember all of our brothers and sisters on the street with whom we may not agree. Like Paul, we are thankful God is being preached, even though we may not understand (them). We pray that as we study the Word together, we will find the truth."

At another time, he prayed, in his Bible study group, that "the street Christians not get bent out of shape" and "We think of our many brothers and sisters we humanly don't agree with. Help us love them."

And, in his day by day routine, even in answering the phone, he keeps insisting on a note of love in the difficult and complex Jesus People movement. He answers his phone: "Jesus Loves you, Speaking."

Pederson's own frustration and anxiety—and moderateness—perhaps signals the fact that no one man is going to take it all over. Linda can't do it; she and the Children of God (see next chapter) can't do it; the evangelists can't do it. The man at the hub who controls the biggest Jesus People publishing venture and who makes the scene at the festivals is a man without a country, literally without any committed following. The point of correlation—with power—has not come. It may come, at least in part, as concepts of power, now denounced, and concepts of responsibility mature.

III

The role of leadership in the Jesus People movement is one of the most interesting aspects of the whole phenomena. They are training many leaders of their own. Any evangelist now on the top of the anthill of the movement could well watch out. Perhaps already more than 1,000, possibly 2,000 or 3,000, young men have gone through the excellent training ropes of being entrusted *pro tem* with the responsibility for running a small commune. They have had to cope with internal administration, snotty noses, city ordinances, entrenched status quo leaders in the church and out, irate parents, adolescent tantrums and depression, landlords, neighbors, plumbers, bill collectors; they have developed their charismatic talents that enabled them to be selected by their small groups as leaders in the first place; they know where it's "at" and many of them have it together.

Their role in Christianity is not that of looking up to a senior pastor, a youth director, a Sunday-school superintendent. They are leaders of the church. Laymen. Unordained. In the past, such a young person might have picked up a little training in a church Sunday evening youth group as a president or program chairman under the aegis of the professional staff or some patronizing adult.

Now the some 800 Jesus houses have their own indigenous leaders, chosen by the inhabitants, and these young leaders are developing and growing. The Jesus People movement—and Christianity—are inheriting an army of leaders. They develop different styles of leadership. For example, the leader at Oracle House in San Francisco's Haight-Ashbury district is a sort of friendly but go-around-in-circles sort whom his members don't take too seriously, and his role is like that of a mother hen—he tries not to say much but has to nip at his brood, many of them still in bathrobes and nightgowns and pajamas until midmorning. During a breakfast of English muffins and honey, he verbally thumps a brother who gets up and walks around during grace. Later in the girls' commune, the second story of the duplex, during a communion rite with a solid unleavened little wheat loaf on the sunlit floor, he has to admonish another to "think on the Lord" as the brother nonchalantly fiddles with a window during the prayers.

At Maranatha House in Vancouver, British Columbia, a dark house atop an overgrown hill of unkept brush, the main job is to put out a newspaper, and midday you find people moping around petting their dogs and plugging in coffee pots, not planning much for the rest of the day. Then again, Craig Wakefield, Portland, has his all-men group together early at the House of Joy (assisted by songster-saint Troy, whom we met earlier). Elder Marty Irvine of the twenty-three-member House of Life in Buffalo, New York, has his brood up at 6:15 A.M. for a quick breakfast followed by an hour of prayer and Bible study, and then everybody is out, either to jobs or day-long witnessing. Up toward Alaska, on 150 acres on the north shore of Shuswap Lake, 325 miles north of Vancouver along the Trans-Canada Highway, Robert and Marlene McGoran, both twenty, and four others in their Jesus commune are up at six A.M. milking goats, collecting eggs, gardening, working the horses, etc.

The four elders at Smyrna House in Toronto indulge in no recreation as such (they do have interesting hobby-vocations—art work, electronics, etc.). The Jesus People at Berachah Farm, near Petaluma, California, fifty miles north of San Francisco, hop in their little bus about every other day for some kind of trip. They may go to argue with the cultish Children of God who have moved to a town north of them, or more likely than not they ride down to the beach. Sometimes they travel along the coast for a holiday at Big Sur or somewhere else. The point is, each leader has his own show. Each leader tends to be about the same age as his constituents. Most of the big-wig manipulators, such as George Bogle in Detroit, live away, often in a new, expensive area, although they may spend a lot of time around the commune broadcasting, etc. But the communes are not so dependent on these men as the latter would like to think. While reminding one of a Father Divine or Daddy Grace in their one-man efforts, the big outside leaders know full well that the houses are pretty much in the hands of the youth and their own selected leaders. Even when one lives in, as Russ Griggs does with Meissner's inspired Jesus People Army in Vancouver, he can live in only one place. Griggs and his wife live as house parents in one of the women's communes. Usually some youth is handling all the problems of doctrinal differences, plumbing and community relations in the diverse locations.

A prime feature of the whole Jesus People scene, says the Rev. Donald M. Williams, is the fact that "this spiritual outburst is student led." Williams is minister of college students at the Hollywood Presbyterian Church, just north of Hollywood and Vine. He has a Ph.D. from Union Seminary and Columbia University. He launched the big coffee house, Salt Co., at his church, a commune, Virgil House, and other projects. About Jesus People leadership in general he said, "The initiative has passed from the professional Christian worker, be he pastor, youth leader, or campus ministry staff member. . . . In an era when students have led the protest against war and racism, we should not be surprised that they have taken the Gospel of Christ and moved it into their world. Tens of thousands evangelize today rather than just a few paid professionals." Further, he notes, "This student leadership is emerging out of the youth culture with integrity." [6] They are not going to be assimilated by well-heeled adults nor forced into prescribed roles.

The young men will arrive in their thirties and forties with more parish training and practical Christian experience than many archbishops and more rounded experience than many specialized but limited pastors. Young preachers turned on to Jesus People go out and win hordes; for instance, Richard Hogue, twenty-four, racked up 2,950 reported conversions and 604 baptisms in his SPIRENO (Spiritual Revolution Now) crusade in Houston, and a new preacher in the Detroit area, 21-year-old Frank Majewski of Warren, Michigan, who had a life before conversion that would compare with anything in *A Clockwork Orange,* packs 700 youths into the social hall of a Catholic church on Fridays, with no strings tied to the church.

Already the influence is felt as youths are being given key jobs on church boards. A sixteen-year-old, Barry Gruebbel, was named a deacon and head usher at a United Church of Christ parish in Dallas, and sixteen-year-old Mike Mathes was named deacon of a Presbyterian church in Little Rock, Arkansas. Fourteen-year-old Fred Hartwick beat out two attorneys, an insurance man and a woman pillar of the church to win a spot on the twelve-man vestry of his Episcopal church in San Francisco.

The new form of leadership training could supersede to a great extent the work of main-line seminaries. The Children of God, the Jesus People Army, the J. C. Power and Light Co. and the Hollywood *Free Paper* all have training sessions. They aren't all they are cracked up to be, however. The Jesus People Training Center, advertised in Pederson's Hollywood *Free Paper,* was defunct. When applications for registration were sent in response to ads for 1971 summer sessions, registration checks were cashed without advising the senders of cancellation or informing them that they were being assigned to other sessions and meeting places than the ones for which they had applied. I applied under the name H. H. Ward, with a fake address and fake recommendations. All I have to show for it is a canceled $10 check. No acknowledgment. Nothing.

The Jesus People approach may lead into a type of training already being practiced by the "seminary of the streets" sparked by Dr. Gerald Taylor, a New York psychiatrist and Episcopalian, under the auspices of heavily endowed Trinity Episcopal Church, near Wall Street and Greenwich Village. Taylor notes that Jesus pivoted his work not in institutions but among the "inhabitants of the highways and byways, the fields and the villages," or in the modern times, the "streets." "The regular system tends to put you in a model that doesn't work any more," said Kevin Martin, twenty-four, of Dallas, according to an Associated Press report. In place of his third year at Berkeley Divinity School in New Haven, he is substituting work at the street seminary. "What we get in the streets is much more helpful in preparing for the ministry," he said.[7]

Possibly the new young men will do for the church what fledgling merger plans such as the Consultation on Church Union have tried to do with traditional leadership—bring new forms, unite ministries and congregations and shape a viable church for the future under the new younger leadership. "The pluralism which Jesus People accept among themselves indicates the urgent need for the church to break down walls of separation. It points to less structured, more *ad hoc* ecumenical activities for churches in the future." [8] No wonder that some keen church theologians, wary if not discouraged at current movements to unite the church and worried about the boredom of the ecumenical efforts in parlors and sanctuaries, look out of a corner of their eyes with hope at the Jesus People, despite differences from their own styles. Although the Rev. Dr. Ronald E. Osborn, professor of church history at the Christian Theological Seminary, Indianapolis, is concerned about the possibility of "a self-righteous sectarianism" winning out as it has in church history with the start of new groups, he nevertheless concedes the Jesus People movement may emerge as "possibly a source of new and committed leadership to a rejuvenated Christian cause."

The Rev. Dr. Eugene Carson Blake, architect of the fledgling COCU merger scheme, which he left to less charismatic hands as he went on to become general secretary of the World Council of Churches in Geneva, tells me that by the end of the next decade "I expect that many young people touched by the Jesus movement will be positive contributors to the life of many Christian congregations throughout the United States."

Dr. Lorena Tinker, a research associate at Washington University, St. Louis, who worked on a seven-volume report on the dynamics of conflict (and whose own children, wearing peace arm bands in a Des Moines school in 1965, became the basis for a milestone U.S. Supreme Court decision), said, "Professional leaders will use every trick in the bag, like calling them sinners, to keep the kids. The kids are now licking their wounds, and enjoying it.

"But the kids have more cultural tools than the professional religious adult leader," she said, "and can outwit the professional. Between the professional leader and the kids, a day of reckoning is coming."

4

Apostles of Faith or Fear:
Children of God

The Jesus People movement can be measured against the cultish Children of God, originating in Texas, and now spread out in small numbers across the nation and into Canada. They are so radical, so narrow, so wrapped up in themselves, so exclusive, so bent on overwhelming all in their way, that they stand out from moderates, much like end-of-the-world, extreme cult groups have always stood out in history. Radicals such as Thomas Munzer, with his belief in immediate revelation, and Jan Mathys, apocalyptic terrorist, left little personal legacy in the sixteenth century but added to the turmoil that challenged the monolithic Lutheran Reformation.

I

The Children of God, who of all the Jesus People are most likely to become a denomination, (if they aren't one already, because of their efficient organization and single mindedness,) are forcing behavior patterns and reactions that determine style in other Jesus People groups. By summer of 1971, they looked more like a threat than a strange cult. Chatting with Linda Meissner and Russell Griggs of the Jesus People Army, I suddenly learned that they also were throwing in the towel to join up with the Children of God. This may not be a fair way to put it, but the joining of what I consider two temperamentally different wings of the Jesus movement means that something already is wrong.

You found, then, a sort of triumvirate in the Jesus People Army headquarters in Seattle. There was the JPA commander, Linda Meissner. Sitting with her was the JPA field captain for Canada, Russ Griggs, and listening in and adding his views was "Jethro," an import from the Children of God training camp at a ghost town near Thurber, Texas. You almost never can learn the name of a member of the Children of God, for that would be an ego trip taking glory away from God. Jethro says of his own name, "I forgot." (Actually he is John Treadwell, married to founder David Berg's daughter, Linda "Deborah" Treadwell.) Jethro, twenty-six, former director of the central colony in Thurber, used to be a computer programmer and IBM consultant. He had three years of college.

The significant thing is that Griggs's Vancouver operation was not merely a drop in the bucket. His JPA has an eighty-acre ranch, a bakery-delicatessen near downtown Vancouver, a remedial school for high-school dropouts accredited by Canadian officials, a coffee house, Shepherd's Call, and boys' and girls' separate communes. Not a small thing at all. And one of the biggest organizations in the Southeast U.S., the House of Judah, two other communes and a farm of David Hoyt in Atlanta were also joining up with the secret, seclusive but hard-hitting Children of God.

Griggs explained why his group was joining. "We had a high casualty rate of dropouts, and we wanted to devise ways to keep them." Starting the school was one way. Linking arms with the Children of God was another. "We were one of the strongest because we were well organized, but we would only have 50 per cent with us still after a year. Others would have a lot less. But the Children of God would only have about a 15 per cent casualty rate. We sent twenty-five of our leaders to their leadership training center in Thurber. We all merged. I am director in Vancouver."

The total membership of the JPA and Children of God in the Northwest in the actual families or communes is 250, Griggs said. It was the world evangelism program of the Children of God, Griggs added, with their excursions to Europe and elsewhere (the newest work is in Amsterdam, Holland) that appealed to the Jesus

People Army. In addition, "They have a system of communication far superior, and a training program." He gave as an example the ham radio system between the Children of God communes and an ordered daily correspondence between the communes. "We'd get together once in a few months," said Griggs of JPA intercommunication. He sees the alliance, or merger—each group still retains its identity and autonomy (although this remains to be seen)—as an opportunity to reach out. "We are interested in starting new colonies instead of patching old ones. But we will develop work totally autonomously."

Ideologically, the two—JPA and Children of God—had a lot in common, if not in temperament. "We are opposed to working for money—so are they," said Griggs. Said Linda, "If you are an officer, you have to be ready to move. There is more in the Children of God than the typical Jesus freak. They are fulfilling the Great Commission. We're revolutionaries. It's not business as usual. God is love. We need a revolution of love."

They are revolutionaries, both the JPA and Children of God. They may differ in style at points, but both are the yippies of the movement. Outside the system. Once you understand this, you see what the two have in common. You also see some of the reasons for the friction stirred so universally by the Children of God. The friction is caused by "being outside it all" while on the inside with God. The end justifies the means for the Children of God. They do not hesitate to bite the hands that feed them. Hence the conclusion of the previous chapter that the oldsters and benefactors are not going to take over the Jesus People. The secrecy probably causes the most friction—plus the intense study approach. Parents who lose contact with their children feel that their young people are coming under some hypnotic influence. Most criticized by parents is the name change and loss of identity. They call up looking for a son or daughter, and Children of God phone answerers feign to know nothing about them—"There's only Abraham, Rebekah, Priscilla, Barnabas, etc. here," they say. Also, the youths empty their bank accounts and take all physical possessions to the commune for disposal. It is a strange feeling to watch the newcomers stack up hundreds of records, portable TV's, bicycles, radios—as I watched one night at the Children of God commune in Los Angeles. A truck takes everything away for a quick sale. Parents, distraught at the clean-out of possessions, the dropping out often from school or a good job, get beside themselves when the kids are secreted away and they are refused entrance. Linda had not kept her JPA so secret, but she does not object to the style of the Children of God. Concerning the secrecy, Linda tells one, "It's no different than going to boot camp or Princeton. They are on a trip like everyone else. There are teeny differences, but we have majored on minors too much. It (secrecy) is just a minor thing." About the Children of God's alleged negativism toward others: "Some people try to be too broad," Linda says of the critics. "The Children of God do not believe they are the only way. They'd be foolish to do that." But does she believe they are on the right track? "I sure do," says Linda.

Here's how the merger story was turning out in late spring of 1972. Linda had totally disappeared from the scene. She had been reported to be in London, and also in Los Angeles, according to John Salvesen, her fireman husband of two years. John, for his part, had begun fighting the Children of God tooth and nail.

"She thought she was another Apostle Paul," Salvesen told me sadly. "She's really out of it. Like a schizophrenic, she's two people." Her parents heard from her at Christmas 1971, when she asked for money. That also was the last time that Salvesen heard from her. He said he was filing for divorce, not because he doesn't still love her, but to protect himself against any claims on their property by the Children of God, on the advice of his lawyer. "Our relationship in our marriage was good," he said, "and, sure, I'd reconcile if she got her head back together again. But they [the Children of God] are all spiritual robots, and they turn all into schizophrenics."

Salvesen seems to have won the battle in Seattle. He and helpers "kicked out" the Children from Washington Hall, a former Danish lodge for which Salvesen and another held the lease. He said that at this point the Children do not have more than ten people in Seattle in "two little places." At Washington Hall the fifty kids staying there call themselves merely Jesus People and are under a moderate, Richard Vicknair, twenty-seven. Neither the name JPA nor the name Children of God is mentioned.

The much-heralded camp at Burlington, Washington, taken over by the Children, with nearly 200 occupants at one point, has been trimmed down by law officials who limited occupancy to no more than fifty.

Griggs, who wanted to gain so much (at least statistically) in the merger in Vancouver, seems to have suffered considerable losses. In backing out of the merger with the Children, he rescued only forty of his kids, with the Children keeping 150 in three houses. Griggs also lost the bakery and Shepherd's Call coffee house (see Chapter 1).

II

Who are the Children of God?

The founder of the radical movement was Christian and Missionary Alliance pastor and evangelist David Berg, fifty-three. Berg had left Arizona where he had worked among the Indians. Some people say he was booted out of this work because of differences with the church authorities. Observers say his hostility to the established church began at this time. Berg and his large family of six moved to the Los Angeles area. In 1944, he joined the Reverend Fred Jordan as public relations and front man for Jordan's "Church in the Home" radio program. They worked out of Jordan's "Soul Clinic" building on Los Angeles' skid row. The first rift between Berg and Jordan occurred, observers say, when Jordan told Berg's relatives to vacate a training center ranch in Texas being used for furloughed missionaries. Berg left Jordan at this point, and traveled as a free lance, eventually joining his mother, Virginia Brandt Berg, a radio preacher in her own right, at Huntington Beach, Calif. About this time he published a biography of his mother, without using his name, called *The Hem of His Garment: The Life Story of Virginia Brandt Berg*. Besides the Bible, it is one of the few books which the Children of God can read. By 1968, Berg had acquired a coffee house, once run by Teen Challenge (Dave Wilkerson's group). Here, Berg gathered a small youth following which he called Teens for Christ. In this project, his approach with the Children of God began to form. He urged the youths to live in the coffee house, to quit their jobs, drop out of school, and escape from the grip of the establishment. A "prophecy" that California was doomed sent Berg and his followers to Palm Springs and Tucson. Possibly adverse developments in California led to this departure. An item in the Huntington Beach (Calif.) *Daily Pilot* of May 21, 1969, reads:

A group of sojourning Teens for Christ crusaders today have $2,500 prices on their heads. Arrest warrants were issued for the Christian revolutionaries when their sentence and probation hearing dates came and went Monday, just like April and the great earthquake they feared. The 14 young men and women are presumed to be among a flock led by pastor Dave Berg to Tucson, Ariz., last month. . . . All were convicted April 3 in two separate jury trials of disrupting Costa Mesa High School and Maude B. Davis Intermediate School during a Feb. 17 demonstration against "a Godless educational system."

After eight months of moving about, Berg was again hired by Jordan, who let the growing tribe of Bergs live on his Mingus, Texas, ranch. Sources say Jordan was greatly pleased when the Children fixed up the ranch. While Berg himself began to fade from sight, and has been variously reported as being in England and in Israel, Jordan provided the growing movement with the six-story former rescue mission down the street from his Soul Clinic. Jordan began to make capital out of the children on his TV programs, as he showed them to viewers, told of their change from drugs to Jesus, and asked for funds. He then opened a 110-acre date and fruit ranch at Coachella, Calif., called it "The Children of God Ranch," and sought to raise a half million dollars through his TV programs and mailings. This was only one of several projects launched by Jordan. When the Children began directly to question Jordan's using them, the inevitable rift began. This all came to a head, some people say, when the elder at Coachella complained to Jordan that the Children were allowed to use only ten of the 110 acres while Jordan was giving the impression in his fund raising that the whole project was for the Children of God. As a result of this confrontation, or at least following it, the Children were booted out of the three properties run by Jordan. Some insiders say the Children could have stayed in the Los Angeles location, but left all three houses in protest.

Theodore Patrick, community relations staffer for California Gov. Ronald Reagan, has a more sordid account of the reasons for the departure. Patrick, who has been fighting with the Children since his own son had a run-in with them on a California beach, claims that Jordan tried to get him fired by Governor Reagan. When Jordan failed in that, Patrick said, Jordan feared the law would crack down on him. Patrick said he received a peace letter from Jordan. He said Jordan was running scared after the parents' organization was launched and feared ending up in jail along with the Children of God. Also, the activities of the Children of God as family breakers, now clearly in evidence, were very much in opposition to the views of the right-wing clientele which Jordan had consistently milked on his radio and TV programs.

III

I had heard all kinds of rumors about the Children of God; once you get in you can't get out, etc. It was one of the first places I decided to go into in disguise, as I began the early part of my research in Los Angeles. I suppose I could have found them in a park, got converted, testified, and let them take me back that way. I preferred to play it straight, not too sure how good an actor I would be in the more dramatic situation. I knocked on the side door but was refused entrance. It was not open to outsiders, I was told. I hung around outside anyway, and as a group was leaving to witness, one of them told me to come back later that night and somebody would let me in. I was kind of an enigma to them, for I am tall, bearded, a little older than they and had a vague story when they asked "What do you do?" and "Are you saved?"

They were good to me, despite the fact that their building was locked up tight against types like me coming off the street in skid row. They revel in the beach-acid-heads, highschoolers, college dropouts, runaways. Immediately when they let me in, they rushed to me and popped a sandwich into my hand. "You must not have eaten for a week," one thin faced man sighed, relieved that I accepted the sandwich. And, "Look at him, man, he must be hungry." But the truth of the matter is I had just had a full bottle of wine and enough Italian food at a fancy dinner to feed an army of Hannibals. The sight of food was too much—but my disguise was working. I did look down-and-out, and these youths wanted to feed me. So I managed to get the sandwich down, pretending to be hungry. I could act, after all. Eventually, I was also to get in on the chocolate ice-cream act, with offers of seconds and thirds.

I learned during this experience to tighten up my drifting, no-place-to-go sort of background story, but the bland answer to their "Are you saved?" bit worked beautifully. "Well, I was baptized. I was saved when I was small, but I suppose I have backslid some." They could cope with a real, clear-cut sinner or a new-born-again believer. Unlike the fundamentalists of old, they could not deal with a bland situation, for recognizing as they do the validity of salvation and your own honesty, what else is there to say? The answer from the Children of God is, "Do you want to serve God here?" When I did not agree to that, they had some differences among themselves, and despite a promise of a place to stay for the night, one young late-arriving blond youth decided he would not be happy if I stayed, since I wasn't going to serve God there. The leaders apparently didn't really care. But this fellow had his opinions. By 3:30 A.M. I was glad to be put out on the street (somebody wanted to know if I had enough for a flophouse around the corner) after seven separate persons had spent the major part of the night trying to convert me. I was glad, too, to get out in light of their plans to sleep until Sunday afternoon, as I had other things to do that Sunday. Leaving the commune is supposed to be a problem with the Children of God—once you get in, they are supposed not to let you out. I was testing this, and they were putting me out at that ungodly hour. The real test, I suppose, is to be accepted by them, promise to work with them, then try to get out.

Almost universally, the Children of God express deep antagonisms. They revel in the fact that persecution and unpopularity are the marks of being on the right track. They are not just the red sackcloth, ashes-and-rod types you might expect after seeing them warning of doom. They are very happy, jubilant. That's why TV networks, *Time* Magazine, and others have a field day in photographing them. Happy, but, oh, their language. When you sit with them, as a bum or some kind of society dropout, in beard and old jeans and tennis shoes, unknown to them as a reporter, you begin to hear a bunch of "damns" and some other expletives. They come on strong, language-wise, when arguing their faith to other Jesus People. The encounters likely provide a testing for both sides.

The kids from Berachah House, Petaluma, California, usually come back shaken up after an excursion north to Sebastopol to talk with a newly arrived group of the Children of God. "They're pure hate," said Byrne Power, fifteen. "They called us luke-warm pukes," said Dennis Flack, nineteen, who was "almost a member." "For the most part, they go around breaking up houses, using Jesus as an instrument to introduce themselves to naive young people. Jesus is second to them. I was hitchhiking, and they took me in and indoctrinated me. I'd decided I wanted to leave. They didn't want me to leave. The Devil would get me, they told me, if I left." Dennis told of one youth who was forced back after walking six miles to get away, and who then escaped again, successfully walking twenty miles. Mike Miller of the J. C. Power and Light Co., in Los Angeles, said of the Children of God "They have no love and understanding." He included the work of Tony and Sue Alamo in Saugus, California, and the people with them as targets in his criticism. "They say, 'I don't love you, but I tell you to go to hell.' "

IV

As a newsman in Detroit, I've received calls from parents and aunts about the Children of God, and about their secretive and sometimes violent ways. One distraught Birmingham, Michigan, dad had two daughters in the Children of God commune in Detroit. He was not allowed to see them. He recalls, "I've seen parents drag their kids out." He had to go to Cincinnati to get one of his daughters back. Frustrated because members pretended to have no acquaintance with any girl of the name by which her father knew her, he stuck around and watched them break up for assignments, spotted his daughter, and, backed up by a police squad car, trailed her to her street-corner witnessing site. "We came out of hiding, followed the group, slammed on the brakes, and grabbed her."

Mrs. Peggy Justus, an affable, big-hearted lady who tried to get a mission going in Detroit (she is white in a black ghetto, and few attended) near a second-hand outlet run by her husband, had close personal dealings with the Children of God. The Children of God seemed to be one way to reach youths—black and white, Mrs. Justus thought. She said at last bitterly over dinner one day, "I was the only sucker" among those trying to work with Jesus People. "But I was sincere."

Here is her story as she told it:

When I first saw these young people on the Phil Donahue Show on TV, I thought, wow! These kids are for real. Their singing and bright smiles won my heart, and in less than a month I had written them and invited them to come to Detroit (from Cincinnati) to a mission that I had here.

They did arrive in late March, 1970. There were fourteen of them, about eight boys and six girls. They had traveled in two old cars and were tired. Dirty and hungry. They had no earthly possessions except what each one carried in a small bag or roll on his back. They had a couple of beat-up guitars. But they seemed to be quite happy. They stayed in my home a couple of nights and then decided they would all like to sleep at the mission.

And so over to the mission we went. The boys sat on the pews that we had labored so hard to buy. They put their boots up on the pews in front of them and lay back in the pews. They hated the church look of the mission. And the first thing they said was that the pews had to go. They wanted colored fluorescent lights and rugs on the floor. The microphone and PA system were turned up so loud you could hear it two blocks down the street. Well, that was the beginning of the Children of God in Detroit.

After that there were a lot of sleepless nights for me. Irate parents were calling me at all hours concerning their children. When new kids came into the movement, they were taught three things immediately: (1) forget education even if you are supposed to graduate tomorrow; (2) forget parents (Mt. 10:26; Lk. 14:33); (3) Don't work—the system is not where it's at. With these three basic steps, they capture almost any kid. This is what he wants to hear.

These kids are so extreme and so far-out. They have a radical, extreme concept of Christian living. And talking about Christian living, I didn't see too much of that among them. They used profanity continuously, until I had to tell them to stop. They lie and deceive people. Business people have donated printing presses, copy machines and all kinds of printing equipment to these kids because they have led them to believe that they have a drug program. They have no drug program as society knows it. We know, of course, that God can deliver people from drugs, but they deceive people to think otherwise. In general, it has been a nightmare.

There were so many street fights with parents who were trying to get their children to come back home and finish school, keep their jobs, etc., police had to send scout cars many times. And some of the neighbors told me that they were planning to get up a petition to get these kids off the street and out of that house.

Mrs. Justus said she was turned off, too, by the presence of army deserters and worried of complicity under the law.

It made no difference if you were a deserter from the Army, Navy or Air Force. They had complete disregard for all authority, all laws of the land, civil or parental, if you were in the army of the Lord. I went as far as I could go. When they first came here, I went with them to talk with the Police Department and ask for their cooperation—I believed in them. I took them to a 5 and 10 cent store of a friend of mine, and he gave them things, but I had to stop the kids—they would have cleaned him out. I took them to the dentist, fed and clothed them. I gave them money. I called worried parents, even out of state, and fought for these mixed-up kids, even in the courtroom [she reports she has put her mission up as bond for one youth who is being examined on a charge incurred before he joined the group]. And I finally wound up being used and ridiculed.

V

Reaction grew in many areas. In Detroit, I began to collect and publish data on the missing youths, after I had worked the other side of the fence, doing an inside study of the operations of the Children of God in Detroit.

The group had rented a two-story dilapidated commune in a dense concrete jungle, a no-man's land just off the main street of Woodward north of the Grand Circus park area. They also had a store-front chairless coffee house with red carpeting and posters of doom, next to a topless show-bar in another sleazy district. And they run a tight operation.

None will admit to leadership, but by their actions you can figure them out. The Detroit leaders now appear to be Simon, who strums and sings and gets the afternoon witnessing trips together, and Malachi, who has to deal with parents and financial matters and overall administration. Regular members are not allowed the luxury of possessing or carrying money. Brimstone, who was serving as guard one night, said in a long rap with me, that he hadn't had any money in his pockets for four months.

The means and method of control are also evident inside. Original parent-denouncing, claim-the-land revolutionary songs, proclaiming Jesus as lord and master, constantly play over loud-speakers in all the rooms, much like the technique of brain-washing, Peking style.

Every action is monitored. Following the Biblical injunction to go out in twos to witness (Mk. 6:7), the Children of God members are even accompanied to the bathroom door by a buddy.

They are so conditioned that even when you step on an unsuspecting body sleeping in a narrow hallway as you exit early in the morning, the body groans and says in its sleep, "Praise God."

Malachi is Dave Luevano, twenty-two, of West Des Moines, Iowa, "saved" in Fort Worth three years ago. He looks like thirty-five or so. Simon, twenty-three, who does not give his name, is from San Ysidro, New Mexico. His dad, he said, who died four years ago, was a former clerk-typist at the White Sands Missile Range.

Both Simon, who is black, and Malachi, who is white, are sentimental about their own mothers, who cried, they said, when they joined the Children of God. They both are still in touch with their mothers, they say, and Simon says his mother has donated her house to help out the movement.

Simon has one of the few beards in the commune. He is married and the father of a small baby. His wife is attractive and an avid dancer and seems to go about keeping her own counsel with an air of independence. One escapee said he went into the movement because he liked Simon. The youth said he regarded Simon as a Martin Luther King type and still does. Most are critical of Malachi.

Escapees say they were taught to hate their parents. The alienation toward the home is underscored even in the Children of God

mail system. One envelope on the commune wall says COLONY—
this is mail going to one of the other colonies. The other big
envelope says EGYPT. EGYPT mail is mail going home to parents.
Egypt, of course, in Bible terminology is synonymous with "bondage," as Moses led the Children of Israel out of bondage in Egypt.

Communicating with home is rare, and the lack of effort to do
so is explained sometimes by the youths as "I'm too heavy into
the Bible." And even communication can be a terrifying experience.

Mrs. Marci Guenther, whose seventeen-year-old sister's exact
whereabouts in the movement has remained a mystery, reports an
indirect phone report concerning her sister. Mrs. Guenther is the
wife of Harmen Guenther, twenty-nine, who is national president of the parents' committee to Free the Children of God
(FREECOG). A trained stenographer, she put down what was
said:

> The man calling had a voice revealing some age. I would estimate he
> was in his forties or early fifties. It was not the voice of a young man.
> There was no discernible accent and no background noise of any kind.
> The man has not been heard from since.
>
> MAN: Hello. I'm looking for someone named Marsha.
>
> MARCI: You found her. This is she; what can I do for you?
>
> MAN: My name is brother Joe and I have a letter for you from your
> sister and . . .
>
> MARCI: Wait a minute! You have a letter from me to her or her to me
> or . . . ?
>
> MAN: Just shut up and listen: "I am well and happy. Feel free for the
> first time in my life. The men [detectives] interfering with my family
> [commune] are treating me like a criminal. If they don't leave me alone
> they are going to send me to another state. I am coming back when I
> am ready. Tell them to leave me alone." Click.

Rob Notman, eighteen, son of a Flint, Michigan, stockbroker,
the valedictorian of his Southwestern High, Flint, and an A-plus
student in the summer of 1971 at the Interlochen Music Camp in
northern Michigan disappeared from the campus of the University
of Michigan. His father reports he received a call from his son
later saying he was with the Children of God but would not say
where. He gave a box number where his things could be sent. The

only clue to his whereabouts, says his father, was a sizable cancelled check made out to the Children of God.

Malachi, asked about missing youths and complaints of parents allegedly being lied to, said, "If a parent wants to see his child, we won't interrupt." He said he honestly doesn't know where all the kids are sometimes, and parents won't take No for an answer. He acknowledged that the Children of God had poor public relations, which he said he wanted to improve. "We make mistakes. The Apostles in the Bible made mistakes. But I'll be honest with you. The parents—they're possessive. They have a child around nineteen years, and they want to continue to control his life."

VI

How do the Children of God get the young people, and keep them? Let's take a look at actual Children of God contacts with youths at the University of Michigan Diagonal, the central court of the University, and hear testimonies from two escapees.

The group had worked first primarily in the Wayne State campus area, Detroit, but found greater success at University of Michigan, Ann Arbor. Malachi conceded that a reason might be the greater affluence of the students. Just as the well-heeled suburbanites in Bloomfield Hills end up in churches because, as one Bloomfield pastor pointed out, they have everything else, so it may be with the youths, too. Seeking meaning that materialism can't provide, the more affluent student, more often than not from suburban Detroit or a home outstate, may have the same need as his parents. Critics also say the affluent student aids the movement, for almost without exception, within hours sometimes, the new convert is brought to his bank to withdraw funds and one of the members shows up with him at his home to claim other possessions, such as guitars.

Here's what it was like for Cindy (not her real name). A girl with beautiful long curly hair, she sat on a divan in a long maxi, beneath seascapes in her dad's $150,000 Bloomfield Hill, Michigan, home, as she explained life inside the Children of God commune.

She was dragged out bodily by her father, against her will, but now is thankful, much like one bent on suicide is thankful when the suicide attempt fails and one is rescued.

She was "saved" spiritually in a separate experience one week before running into the Children of God and was looking for a fellowshiping experience. She hitchhiked with a friend to Ann Arbor and met Olympos and Judah, a slight, quiet little man with a mustache. "I didn't use wisdom. We just joined." She was loaded into a van for return to Detroit. "I was looking for a way to serve God and to do God's perfect will."

But, at first, in the colony, she recalls: "I felt terror, pure terror. I refused to go to their meetings for the first two or three days." The songs of hate against parents turned her off. "Look at the way they raised us; they think their money has amazed us. . . ." And hatred against the United States and the system: they would shout, in revolutionary ferver: "Claim the land. . . ."

"I went into hysterics. This is Satan."

Among the chants: "My family (Children of God)—right or wrong!" and "Jesus Christ, whether I live or die. Give me just one more soul before I die."

"They seemed like a big snowball rolling like fear. I said to them, 'You act like you're crazy out of fear.' But they countered everything with Scripture of one sort or another."

She stayed, she said, because "I was searching for God." The appeal was that it was a "place of refuge, food (they get a lot of free ice cream from dairies), a place of fellowship, being with people who claim they love you, and people are around you all the time. It is an easy way out. People are afraid of the world."

She described her leaders as having "eyes glowing like little coals" and "You should have seen me. I was like a robot of steel. I couldn't cry." The only violence she encountered was the "violence when Dad came to drag me away and I screamed." She feared being committed to an institution.

She had a premonition of getting out that day. She was up early, found her lost sandals, "got my Bible," and "paced for two hours over bodies—I stepped on arms and legs here and there, and there was no sound. I even stole some doughnuts, and I thought, 'Am I crazy, stealing doughnuts from Jesus?' " Simon came and told her to come out front. When her parents grabbed her, she said, "It seemed like I flew to the car. I don't remember my feet touching the ground. I sang psalms and cried all the way home. My mind felt like a little reel of tape, so wound up."

She recalled how the Children of God were always drumming her with soft voices and believes she was in a hypnotic state most of the time. "They would do anything. They are so much like the Manson cult; most of them would kill, I believe, if ordered. They will drop God and Jesus out sometime in the future and become revolutionary and kill. It's terrifying to think about it."

Tom Turner, twenty-one, son of a Detroit General Motors tool maker, was in for only three days. Also visiting Ann Arbor with friends, he was approached by the Children of God and asked if he wanted to know Jesus. He was taken to a room in a building at Ann Arbor where they prayed over him. Malachi read, he says: "We are at war, we pledge ourselves totally against the system." Two days later, not hearing from Tom, his mother recalls, "After a frantic morning of phoning police departments in Ann Arbor and also hospitals, I was out of my mind with worry! Then Tom called me after lunch and said he was living at the commune of the Children of God, and that he had been 'saved.' A Reverend David Luevano [Malachi] then took over the phone, saying we had a fine son, and that he would come home shortly afterward with two members in a Toyota pickup truck to get his clothes and 'worldly goods'—electric guitar, folk guitar, amplifier and speaker box— about $1,000 worth of equipment. . . . They left quite hurriedly, and I thought Tom looked very tired and in a daze. My husband came in about fifteen minutes later—rushing home early from work, thinking he could stop him. We didn't know what to think!"

When trying to phone his parents that first time, Tom said, "Malachi grabbed the phone and fed me words." He said he was not allowed to see his friends when they came. They were told he was asleep.

Later, his friends went back. "They saw Tom sitting inside, looking bug-eyed, as if he were drugged on something," his mother continued. "Many of the others looked just like him— drugged or hypnotized. They tried to talk to Tom, but couldn't communicate with him. There was always a member hanging onto him. They also saw his equipment on the stage and someone

playing his cherished guitar. They wanted to bring him home—
even had him outside, but the police chased Don [Tom's brother]
and his friends away at that point. Don came home to tell his dad
and me that the bunch had his brother's mind.

"After that episode, my husband and I decided it was time for
action. On August 4, our minister, Robert Duggan of St. James
Presbyterian Church in Detroit, and also a psychiatrist, Dr. Calvin
Hughes, advised us to get him out of that place bodily. We went
to the commune and demanded to see Tom. After ten minutes,
they brought him downstairs to the porch. My husband and I got
a hold of him and did a lot of talking, all the while walking him
to the car.

"The leaders and some members were right behind us. Don
and three others were in another car behind ours, and at that
point, they got out to talk about the equipment. We shoved Tom
into our car and took off. We put Tom in the hospital and Dr.
Hughes ran tests on him immediately for drugs, but nothing
showed up. It was very possible he was given something in his
food that the body assimilates, the doctor said. (Most feel, however, that there is no use of drugs.)

"Tom is still under the doctor's care. The paper he signed,
giving away his worldly goods, is not valid because of the state of
his mind at the time. The doctor said he was on the verge of a
nervous breakdown."

Tom, who had completed three years at WSU as a fine arts
major, was a member of a four-member rock band. He is still
trying to get all his equipment back. The Turners, on advice from
Malachi, they said, went to Cincinnati to seek the equipment.

But once down there, the Children of God in Cincinnati "were
really hostile and mad when we dropped by, and said they had no
phone call from Malachi as we had been told."

Tom is also mad now that his hair was trimmed. "They told us
it would help us look pretty for our parents, like Bible students.
They taught us to hate."

VII

Is it true, as has sometimes been charged, that the Children of
God have been hypnotized?

Simon, spokesman for the seventeen-member commune at 31 Charlotte, just off Woodward, in Detroit, said any notion of the group's being hypnotized was ridiculous. He said the group was merely following Biblical injunctions to study the Scriptures and witness to others.

Hypnotists, hypnologists, psychologists and churchmen have various opinions.

"In our studies of group action, hypnotism is a definite possibility," said Dr. Dale Cottrill, Ph.D., professor of speech and expert on the psychology of communication at Macomb College, (South Campus) Warren. "The restrictive type of situation poses real possibility of hypnotism. You do not need drugs if you use music and spell binding. Hitler and his youth movement were good examples of this. He used chanting, lighting and repeating phrases."

Harry Kruk, a stage hypnotist in the area for over twenty years and member of the American Society for the Advancement of Hypnosis, emphasized the importance of conditioning for hypnosis. He defined hypnosis, as others also did, as a state of suggestion. He says it is possible that groups such as the Children of God and the India-oriented Hare Krishna consciousness groups make use of this psychic mechanism, whether they are aware of its significance or not.

Another contributing factor, Kruk believes, is to be found in today's social atmosphere. "In time of panic when emotions rule rather than reason, in his insecurity a man may be manipulated to believe anything he is capable of imagining," says Kruk. "His mind is vulnerable and accessible to any hopes, be they true or false. He can be misled by the mentally sick, fleeced and misused by confidence men or again easily led by those who have truly his interest at heart.

"When there is a lack of communication, in the home, in society, a lack of confidence in the individual, his search for identity and security may end by creating them in his imagination rather than in reality, in much the same manner as a drowning man may clutch the sea weed at the bottom of a lake."

A Detroit hypnologist, Mrs. Christine Retzloff, director of the Hypnosis Consultation Center, defines hypnosis as a "level of awareness . . . and suggestibility, but a person must surrender control." She says hypnosis involves alpha brain waves, which are used twice a day as a person goes to sleep or awakens. It is an in-between stage between consciousness and sleep, a very creative stage.

She says, "Groups that enter into ecstasy are very definitely in that stage and could very easily be considered hypnotized. All a group such as the Children of God has to do to hypnotize a person is to get his confidence and relax him. You get his attention by making him afraid."

Children of God are noted for their emphasis on doom. They wear sackcloth in public protests, and sinners and members who question such an approach are warned of the fires of hell.

Mrs. Retzloff suggested that the Children of God may be going through three states in hypnosis. First, the conditioning of fear. "Is there anything more effective than fear? Most people go to work out of fear of poverty, etc." Asking "Are you saved?" is a fear technique.

Second, the alpha level is achieved by overwhelming a person in the group. "A person in this state has surrendered control of his mind. He is relaxed to this level and is willing to follow." Says Mrs. Retzloff, once you are trapped by fear or similar emotions and reduced to the alpha level, you reach the state where "you can be manipulated."

Not all explain the control as hypnosis. James Adams, dean of students and professor of psychology at Moody Bible Institute, Chicago, tells the *Free Press* that the Children of God may be no more than a normal reaction of youth in the counterculture as they reject the past and parents who hold no meaning for them.

"It's not a form of hypnosis, but a form of reaction," he said. In fact, he feels there is less conditioning in the movement than in much of the rest of society. "But there is a mutual interest among the Children of God in a type of conformity that is less rigid, but that nevertheless creates its own control."

"It's too easy to view them as a strange or different kind from others," said Jerome Heckenmueller, who teaches social psychology and measurement at the University of Detroit. "There might be a difference of degree and nonsocial behavior, but there is a great deal of similarity between their behavior and that of traditional groups."

He noted that in such movements one loses some of his individual qualities in "mass hysteria and hypnosis and crowd behavior. As one engages in the group about him, his behavior becomes that which he would never do on his own."

VIII

With all of the negative reports on the Children of God, it is still hard to escape their charm, particularly in certain respects. To a routinized, affluent culture and its boring institutions, they offer the drama of action and a method of confrontation and contrast. The results often provide their own authentication.

Among the more positive work is that of the Ellenville, New York, commune. Some observers wonder if it is perhaps one stage removed from the original main-line Children of God. Nevertheless, parents are still, at this writing, coming in and pulling out their kids. In Ellenville, about ninety-five miles north of New York City, the Children of God thing is together in a former Jewish day camp, which has also served as a state-aided drug rehabilitation center, now moved on down the road. The Children of God are so crowded here that in their all-night rock band sing-along the kids don't have room to dance. They settle for holding hands, waving their arms in ecstasy and shouting the usual "Praise God" and "Amen."

The movement here has less emphasis on escaping the "system." The members are even accepting assignments in churches, and their chants and songs are positive. Unlike the "claim the land" and other revolutionary cries in some colonies, such as the one in Detroit, their wonderful songs proclaim a new spiritual birth. Yet I must say that here they knew they were talking to a reporter. In some colonies, such as in Woodland Park, Colorado, a "Selah" light (a night-light bulb) flashes on and off as a warning when parents and other visitors are around, and the right songs are sung accordingly.

No musical in New York matches an evening with the Children of God bands, despite what one might think of their ideology. I asked Amasa (Larry Bisman), a Jewish convert who once played in *Fiddler on the Roof* in Houston, about the possibility of the Children of God going on the stage in New York. "It would have to remain very radical," he said.

But even radical, the spiritual songs are particularly beautiful: "Oh, it's a new morning, oh it's a new morning, yeah, new morning today . . . we love you, Jesus, we love you, Jesus, yeah, oh, we love you, Jesus, we love you right now, la, la, la, la, hallelujah . . . the sun is shining in my heart . . . we love you."

Jared, one of four elders in charge, clean shaven and looking as fresh and innocent as a Sunday morning Baptist youth in a small rural town, was cooperative and did not try to box in a reporter as some colonies do. He and others talk to you softly about Jesus, even when you finally hit the sack at 5 A.M.

The group in Ellenville has worked diligently in painting the four buildings that were loaned to them on condition that they pay the $200 taxes each month. They also are digging trenches for rewiring, conducting a carpenter shop and photo lab.

They call themselves the New England Christian Youth Association and their Bible sessions they call the New England Bible College. In Detroit the Children of God answer the phone as the Inner City Christian Youth Foundation. It may all mean that the Children of God are "going underground," as one member told me, as they put on "all kinds of nice fronts" to deceive people.

The different, positive style in Ellenville, however, may mean that the movement is splitting up and going many ways, and in some new directions with strength.

The Children of God—and their cultic, almost rigid, denominational structure—are significant for the haste with which they make others act and jell their positions. They are important not only in themselves, but as a part of the on-going process, as one agent in a dialectic of opposing views, through which a new culture consciousness is striving to be born.

5

Can Social Action Come From Jesus Freaks?

Jesus People are photographed with their hands and heads raised up to heaven, estatically. They have their arms around one another, tearful with joy, as they come dripping out of the ocean baptismal waters.

Ask them about the future, and many will say "Jesus is the only future. The Lord is coming back at any time." Social concern pales when one's first concern is himself and his own salvation and his second is the salvation of others. All of it in reference to another world instead of this one.

Ever see a picture of a new young Jesus saint handing a piece of bread to a man on the street? Or serving a bowl of soup? Or a sandwich? Have you ever seen a picture of an angelic Jesus youth sleeping on the floor while a transient sleeps in his bed or sleeping bag? Ever see a picture of Jesus People in a court, standing up for a person in trouble?

The observer does not see many overt signs of social action. European theologian Jurgen Moltmann remarked to me in a late night interview in a Kalamazoo, Michigan, student bar that the Jesus People appeared to lack a sense of symbolic action and that they need to take some risks in a larger arena. "Let them preach the gospel and perform symbolic acts," he said. But, he added, merely "eating honey and locusts" like John the Baptist and living an ascetic life is not enough. Symbolic, he said, would be such actions as "throwing dollar notes into a bank or some place and saying 'Money is dead.' "

The Jesus youth, for whom faith is individual, feel they are on the receiving end of God's grace and mercy personally. And they seek to share his grace. But how about the shared money, shared food, the kind word for the sick, the care for the orphans and widows—in other words, the things that St. James said were necessary in the long run for real and undefiled religion? (Jas. 1:27).

First, it must be said that despite all the pie-in-the-sky image, the Jesus People came on the scene and continue to do so as a social action people. Their houses are crash pads or hostels for the youthful poor. Particularly where there is money, there are anti-drug counseling, rap lines and clinics. Linda Meissner, the pioneer, began, as we have noted, on the staff of Teen Challenge, the gang-breaking and anti-drug program of David Wilkerson. Morris Cerullo, Tony and Sue Alamo, George Bogle—all the heavies among the adult generation working the Jesus People vineyard look on their work as an alternative to drugs. If the Salvation Army has a reputation for being social-action minded, largely on the basis of looking after alcoholics on skid row, then surely the Jesus People caught up in trying to rescue wrecked youth from drugs, are social-action minded. No other defense is needed. As the Salvation Army has its Harbor Lights and Bowery missions, the Jesus People have Melodyland across from Disneyland in Anaheim. The once prominent theater with a 3,000-seat auditorium boasts among other things a Hotline—a phone service offering help to 1,200 callers a month seeking withdrawal from drugs, help for an OD friend, etc.

There are probably thousands of similar, smaller scale phone services, some tied in with the Jesus People, some projects of Jesus People in cooperation with a church, some just plain church sponsored. Or, at the other end of the spectrum, there is the help given by radical liberal Jesus religionists, such as Richard York's Free Church phone service and other programs in Berkeley. There are Ambassadors for Christ, East Orange, New Jersey; Love Inn, Freeville, New York City; Town Missions, North Kingston, Rhode Island; Young Life, Houston, Texas; Rapline, Farmington,

Michigan; and Youth Unlimited, Washington, D.C., to name just a few. In a sense, these programs for youth and run by youth—conservative, liberal and nominal Christians—form one important segment of the larger Jesus youth movement. And every Jesus People house that prohibits drugs is an anti-drug center of a sort, meeting the needs of homeless, once-addicted youth.

The Jesus People look like social actionists, at least by comparison with their seniors. The adults support the YMCA, but in many areas the Y has delegated its concern with the young adult transient. "It seems that over the years the Y has moved away from dealing with the lower-class youth [hippies] and has provided a second recreation room for the upper-middle-class people," says Wendell Woodthorp and Jim Talley, Church in the Park, Modesto, Calif. "The Jesus movement has filled a gap that was left when the Y stopped providing overnight places for people on the move. Our work is just a small attempt to do what the YMCA did superbly for many years."

I

I have mentioned being fed immediately when, disguised as a bum, I arrived at the Children of God commune in Los Angeles. I remember, too, that in Milwaukee, at the Sheepfold House, Sutton Kinter, a dark-rimmed, intense but happy young man who was keeping the house while most were away testifying, took me into the kitchen, seated me opposite a big vat of hot carrot-potato-beef soup and started dipping. Again, I had already eaten well (at a hotel), but I managed two bowls. Only after I had finished eating did Sutton begin rapping about Jesus.

In Vancouver, where the Jesus People Army had gotten into the bakery business, youths stood on the streets giving away yesterday's bread to the poor. They also have a portable coffee house in Fraser Valley where they give away sandwiches. The Shepherd's Call Coffee House in downtown Vancouver dispensed its food and hot drinks free. This is a pattern repeated across the continent. Agape House in Washington, D.C., gave free food to freaks and bums alike in restaurant-like booths.

In Seattle, Carl Furioso leads his house to pool resources and buy food for feed-ins for 450 persons a month, at two P.M. on Sundays at Blessed Sacrament parish and at 1:30 P.M. Saturdays at St. Joseph's. Furioso is an example of how those who come the tried-and-true route in the Jesus People movement can nevertheless exit from star gazing into heaven and from computer-like worship of the number of converts into practical social action. He was converted two years ago at Arthur Blessitt's His Place on Sunset Strip in Los Angeles after a drug trip; he worked then at Sparks's Christian World Liberation Front God's Love center in Berkeley and then went with CWLF to Seattle where he linked up with Linda Meissner's Jesus People Army. Furioso, a native of Cleveland, who worked in two restaurants in Ann Arbor, Michigan, when he wasn't involved in antidraft and other protests with the SDS, said, "We have to fulfill physical as well as spiritual needs. We have to be a friend. That is one of our main objectives. Also we have to be an example to other Christians. There has to be a balance of the physical and spiritual. It is more than a personal thing. . . . Christ came to fulfill all people's needs." Even Linda Meissner had tried to put social concern into her salvation shock troops: "Right, it's a part of the gospel. We've got to help the people—that's what Jesus did." Her JPA Catacombs building offered a free clothing store. "We take clothing to people. And we send people out with food at pop festivals."

In San Francisco, newlyweds Ruth, twenty-three, and Tim Hobbs, who lived in the Oracle House, the happy carefree commune with little discipline, created their own social concern project. "Tim prayed to have a free store," said Ruth, clad in a long velvet dress just after a communion service. "We realized that helping the poor is a part of the gospel, and that we would blow it all if we did not reach out." The Oracle House, its companion Harvest House, and Rejoice Always (the girls' section) attest to the way the creative houses might go and the fact they can outlive the tightly-run conservative centers. A year earlier in the same district, I had checked up on Clayton House, a three-story, self-centered, very strict pentecostal dwelling of men and women. Their main interest was broadcasting. Now that sixty-five-member house was closed. Instead, nearby Oracle House, which appears to be a loosely run operation, was expanding and reaching out to the poor.

Then there are groups, not strictly Jesus People by orientation, that must nevertheless be considered a part of the new wave. Unity House, on a third floor in the middle north side of Chicago, is an anti-war commune of liberals, among them ex-nuns and former priest students at Loyola University. The nucleus was involved in anti-draft demonstrations at Loyola. An upside-down flag with crosses is painted on an entire wall that leads into their commune. A permanent resident is an ailing bartender past sixty, recovering from a serious operation. A house guest the same night I was there was a militant young black atheist who had a shopping bag full of anti-war and anti-God handouts. The top leaders were away, but the main effort of this group was clearly producing anti-war materials. On the south side, Jim MacKenzie, thirty-one, and his wife, Robin, run The Ark, which is merely a Sunday-school program on Sundays for black neighborhood kids. Jim is a Ph.D. candidate in biophysics studying the viral system in algae at the University of Chicago. The MacKenzies also offer Sunday dinner to their charges.

II

The Jesus People for the most part have not yet discovered the ecology movement as one of Christian social concern. They are as bad in this area as young Christians were in my day. Back then, in Chicago, Youth for Christ kids used to plant gummed stickers announcing rallies at Soldiers Field on car windows and on tables and walls in high-school cafeterias, generally making a mess of things. This lack of concern for the environment has been picked up by Sammy Tippit, a disciple of Arthur Blessitt and James Robinson, Southern evangelist. Tippit and some friends pushed a wheelbarrow of New Testaments from Mississippi to Washington, D.C., where they met Blessitt, who had dragged his cross from the West Coast to the East Coast. Tippit's youths, in his God's Love and Action program out of the House of the Risen Son in the far North Side of Chicago in the uptown area, "go through 100,000 little red stickers a month," he said. The stickers, selling at $1.50

a hundred, include a Bible message ("Repent, trust Jesus," "One way Jesus," "Greatest love Jesus," "True peace Jesus" etc.) and Sam Tippit's name, address and telephone number circling the words and symbols (crosses, fish, world, etc.). Tippit says the orange-red stickers are meant to be a come-on—"Want a red?" (the stickers' "red" color refers to "downers" or barbiturates) but Tippit acknowledges that many of the stickers may go astray and clutter up things.

Consider a report in *The Lutheran,* national magazine of the Lutheran Church in America:

> He [Blessitt] grabs a roll of what he calls "reds"—a synonym in the dope world for depressants or for "downers"—which in this case are red stickers with a peace symbol and a cross and the inscription, "Smile, God loves you." And off he drives to a high school in the San Fernando Valley where he is scheduled to speak. . . .
> On the school grounds, he pastes the red stickers over everything he walks by—lockers, signs, buildings, windows. To every student he meets, he says, "Here, have a red. Are you saved?" or "Hi, do you know Jesus? He's the greatest trip of all." [1]

Pollutors of the grand outdoors were the non-work-minded Jesus youths that flocked to the Garland Hot Springs, long-neglected resort in the snow-capped Wenatchee Mountains of the Cascade Range sixty miles northeast of Seattle. In that setting, when you look up and around, you see the majesty and splendor of God. But when you look at Garland Hot Springs—where the Jesus People lived as the last group of residents in the summer of 1970 and conducted beautiful outdoor weddings and festivals, filling the trees and skies with praise—there is only destruction. They didn't do it all themselves. Snow has caved in the roofs of cabins, and a restaurant owner down the mountains said that neglect had been taking its toll at the site for over a decade. But as the last tenants the young Jesus People added to the growing ugliness of litter and falling buildings. There seems almost to have been a judgmental hand at work in the whole site, as if it were a sort of Sodom and Gomorrah destroyed after neglect. Ironically, the Jesus People symbols are all over—"Noah" on a broken-down bulldozer, "Jesus Loves You," "Jesus is God," etc.

Newly-arrived caretakers of the doomed 41-acre privately owned former resort camp are a newlywed couple, Carolyn, twenty-one, and Craig Skinner, twenty-six. The fire crackled in their one remaining central cabin as they served tea. "People who came here fell in love with Garland and not Jesus. People forgot Jesus," Carolyn said. (Kelly, three, son of Carolyn, hadn't forgotten Jesus. He looked up at this towering, bearded writer and asked, "Are you Jesus?")

Ecology, however, may come into its own among the Jesus People. The Belly of the Whale, an eleven-member commune in Princeton, Illinois, is starting an action center for groups wanting to fight such ecological problems as pollution, Reverend Harold Burkey, its director, says. And in Pontiac, Michigan, Jack Williams, of the House of Prayer, had organized a march of 150 kids to clean up the city on a Saturday.

III

There are some signs the Jesus People are developing wider concerns as they become more deeply involved in specific problems.

Tippit, again following the style of Arthur Blessitt who warred in public headlines against houses of prostitution in Nevada, is conducting a two-fisted fight against moral pollution in Chicago. He and an aide, Lloyd Cole, were arrested for witnessing in the Rush Street night club district of Chicago. Their "Jesus loves you" to strangers was shaking up the night business, owners admitted. Then, said Tippit, "God laid it on my heart to come to the Civic Center Plaza right across from the City Hall and the Mayor's office to pray and to fast with a 7½ foot cross" until the trial date. "It's sickening . . . it's sad . . . in America today when a person can't go out and talk about Christ without being arrested."

The Christian World Liberation Front in its headline-making days in Berkeley also went about trying to crash strip-joints in the Bay area with the gospel. In New York, Paul Bryant, twenty-one, from San Francisco, zeroed in on the erotic book stores in Times Square. He carried a picket sign: "Jesus is the Right Groove, Smut's a Rut" along with other members of his Jesus Mobilization Committee in New York. The part-time Southern

Baptist student at Golden Gate Seminary in San Francisco and former elder of a commune there indicated that his interest was not limited to cleaning up the bookstores, however. He told a New York *Times* reporter: "Problems are evident everywhere—air pollution, social injustice, poverty, everything. We've given up on the traditional methods of solution. They just haven't worked. Christ, I feel, offers the best alternative to meet these problems." [2]

At Venice Beach, the strip of Los Angeles area coastline where a developer in the 1920s laid out a series of water arteries reminiscent of Venice, Italy, the freaks mill about in droves. A rock concert in a park gathers a throng. It is mid-afternoon, but The Way Coffee House in the midst of it all is locked up. A sign says there will be a prayer meeting and rap in the evening. The freaks, however, become scarce in the evening, as the police allegedly harass the youths. You look into the coffee house, and there are empty paper cups in the almost dark room.

Across the walkaway, Steve Clare, twenty-six, a long-haired youth from Pittsburgh, a graduate of the University of California, was distributing literature that calls for saving the area from private developers and hotel buildings. He viewed the Jesus People who sponsor such coffee houses as "irrelevant and abstract, not related to the social situation. They are very superficial, with the trappings of the hip community, but that is all.

"They stay inside and deliver their rap. That is why people are turned off with them, not because of their architecture. They got nothing coming out of there but coffee and doughnuts. The Jesus revolution could relate to welfare and other issues. There is a real need in a community, not an abstract one like Christ or Marx."

He, however, thinks the young people in the Jesus movement might get wise. "People get desperate and reach back to revitalize philosophy to reconstruct lives and heads. Probably it is all short-lived. I don't think they understand, but when they do, they will move away from their teaching." He felt, on the other hand, that Jesus could be very relevant if followed rightly. In the same vein, Kay Wickett, twenty, who was with a Methodist group from Fullerton visiting the Los Angeles scene, remarked about the Jesus People who show up on the Scripps College campus, Claremont, which she attends, "They have real contradictions. They constantly talk it, instead of live it."

The prayers of the Jesus People sometimes reveal a Christian social consciousness, again reflecting the potential if not the real. For instance, at Christian House, Vacaville, California: "Help us lead lives more dedicated to you and do your will"; "Teach us your love—your agape love"; "Teach us daily"; "I pray for the leadership of the country . . . and for the war, be merciful to both sides"; "I pray for unwed loved ones." And in the Scripture-based discussion from I Corinthians 13 and Philippians 3, one member said, "In order to be a stepping stone, we must lay down our lives. If you love him, you love sisters and brothers and you must not try to get in their way or mix them up." And one boy cited Matthew 7:21, "Not every one that saith unto me, 'Lord, Lord' shall enter into the kingdom of heaven, but he that doeth the will of my Father which is in heaven."

They even get some tough direction in such streamlined spiritual settings as Calvary Chapel, Orange County. Rev. E. E. Romaine, associate minister, says, "These [youths] have been rejected by their families, but we do not try to coddle them, but get them on their feet. We give each a couple of bucks and try to get them to be productive human beings, back in school if they are out. We say they can't use the houses (eight) as a hiding place or a crutch."

Asked what benefits ("besides salvation and getting off drugs") the Jesus Movement has, various Jesus People house leaders indicated a social concern. Paul Campbell, elder of the Twenty-Third Psalm House, Nashville, said, "peace, contentment, love, power to help accept others." Ernest Knowlton, elder, His House, Inc., Indianapolis, said, "Our desire is to provide those people an atmosphere whereby they can prepare to return to society as productive members of society." Tom Salter, minister of Encounter Ranch, Grass Valley, California, said, "There is a valid reclamation of an entire subculture lost, not only in a religious, but a practical sense (*i.e.,* productiveness, good citizenship, etc.)."

Many will still answer "Jesus is sufficient," as Paula Brody, deaconess of Hosanna House, Eugene, Oregon, does or say there are no benefits beyond salvation. "Jesus offers life in his forever

family to those who accept him as personal Savior," said Elder
Marty Irvine, House of Life, Buffalo. Meg Dupee, a former
Catholic and a former Pentecostal, of the St. James Community,
rural Portage, Wisconsin, says: "Salvation is an all-encompassing
benefit that continually affects our lives, therefore affecting society.
Other benefits are tied to this." Richard Whitnable, of the same
commune, says, "If you have salvation, what more could you
need?"

But beyond the public image, they are socially conscious—in
the way they treat a down-and-outer as they try to feed him; in
the way they pray for special expertise in the area of loving one
another; or in their whole bag, which includes an anti-drug clinic
and a self-sacrificial trip into some place on their own. It takes
considerable idealism to give up as much as many of these kids
have—all of their possessions in some cases, and if not that, certainly they have sacrificed or mortgaged their future *pro tem*. At
first blush, a cop-out. But listening to them, you hear the anti-
materialistic idealism, the trust in greater forces and causes than
themselves. Of such idealism come great crusades. It is probably
no wonder that the pietism of the Wesleys and to a certain extent
William Booth of the Salvation Army did not stop with pietism
but led to the development of two of the most forward-looking,
social-action-minded denominations in the history of the church.
Pietism is not social idealism, but somehow it is a good seed bed
for a larger concern.

6

Integration in the Jesus Communes

John Woods, twenty-eight, formerly of Brooklyn, New York, once an Air Force sergeant and a former circulation clerk for the New York *Daily News,* is black. The tall, athletic, personable young man and his wife are the only blacks in the twenty-one-member House of Smyrna in West Toronto, Ontario, Canada. John is not the dishwasher, floor cleaner, janitor, black outcast and flunky of the house. As elder, he shares top authority with three others. While others are doing the dishes after dinner, he is off to visit a new coffee house and serve as emissary for the House of Smyrna.

"It never occurred to me, my color," he said, in answer to a question as to how it is to be a black in a predominantly white movement. "Jesus appeared to all. He died for me as he did for white people."

Said a fellow elder of the House of Smyrna, Ken Hollington, twenty-three, a former color photographer and design draftsman for a Toronto area architectural firm, "In the spirit there is no color. It never occurred to me there is any difference between John and me. The spirit puts these differences away."

The Jesus People do have their conflicts and difficulties over race. But the integrationists tend to win out. They put down the hard-liners who appear discriminatory as they relate to this and other issues, such as to the role of women.

I

Consider two bearded leaders of Jesus youth in Detroit. One, Frank Majewski, a barber, preached in parking lots and church halls but did not worry about starting a commune. Another, Ralph Morrison, started his commune, moving around from house to house and to a deserted church basement. His cult group was so tight that the youths, like the Children of God, sought to lose former identities. They reportedly had to check with him for every decision and even for their correspondence to parents when he took a bunch of them west with him (then returned to Detroit). The closed little world of Morrison was put to test one night when he was invited to speak before Majewski's group in a gesture of friendship and solidarity. Majewski regularly held forth before a group of about 300 (now doubled in 1972) in the social hall of St. Sylvester's Roman Catholic Church, Warren. (A former member of that parish, Majewski calls himself now only a "Christian," and though a layman, has done his own baptizing.) That night in Warren—a northeast Detroit suburb that decided it would rather do without federal aid for housing than promise open housing—there were five black girls in the otherwise all-white audience.

The black girls and other youths began responding to Majewski's spirited, humorous style.

"Yes, well, all right . . . yes. Amen," the black girls said constantly, so regularly it threw Majewski off stride.

"Well, everywhere I go adults come up and say I am too heavy," Majewski said, describing how adults bug him for his simple message to the young.

"Well, all right. . . ." the black girls said.

A white freak on the other side of the room, added, "Right on! Right on!"

Everybody laughed, which provided a sort of emotional release valve in what turned out to be a 3½-hour preaching session. Most sat on the floor, some with Jesus slogans on their jackets.

Then Majewski introduced "Brother Ralph," who came up from the back of the room.

"Do you really want to hear what I have to say?" Morrison asked the group. "Jesus doesn't need your hand clapping or your fleshly Amen trip. Some of you are grieving the Spirit of God tonight. Those of you who are guilty of this will pay for it someday. If this had happened in my house, I'd have thrown you all out."

The black girls now remained silent, as did the whites.

"You made me sick," Ralph said, his head band holding back his shaggy locks. "I tell you on the authority of Jesus Christ, you grieved the Spirit! There is nothing wrong with saying hallelujah and praise God, if in the spirit of true worship. But this is the spirit of a fleshly trip.

"Some of you would rather hang onto your little pentecostal emotional trash. A lot of you come here on Friday night for an emotional social thing. Frank is the best evangelist to hit this city, and he pours out his guts to you. I doubt if you pray much before you come . . . some of you have no depth. You know how to hold hands and hug. You do not know what the Bible says about that stuff."

Ralph was interrupted when he said women should never be heard in public. Male voices asked where the Bible said that, and the bearded speaker said he would not discuss such details before the group but would answer questions afterwards.

Among those who rushed to confront him afterwards were the black young ladies, firmly clutching their own Bibles.

"He condemned us because of our color," said Barbara Lee, twenty-two, who works for a Detroit optical firm. "If he had so much love for Jesus, he would know the Bible says there is no male or female among those who believe Jesus."

"The word of God says the woman is to obey and be silent," Ralph countered.

Mary Steele, twenty-two, tall and gentle with the joy of Christ on her face, said, "You say women are to keep silent. If you got Jesus you can't keep silent. Something wrong with you if you think this."

Morrison became silent and declined to respond to the young ladies any more, but just listened.

"If he had so much Jesus, he wouldn't condemn us," said Barbara. "We love everybody."

The girls invited me down to one of their revivals in a small black church and I slipped in there one night, but I couldn't stay long enough to let them know I was there. Here I heard it again, "Well, all right, yes. Amen"—just as they had spoken it so naturally at Frank and Ralph's rapping. I told Frank later that I might not dig everything I heard, but when a bright-eyed youth comes up to me as one did after that meeting in Warren and asked who was for real, I could only say the person who has joy in his heart, the leader who can smile—he's the real one for me. Frank took it to heart, from me or somebody. He went down, I learned, and had a long, long rap with somber brother Ralph. The next week Ralph wasn't back, and Frank very obviously was inviting all of the women to give testimonies. The blacks did not get back, but they had won—they, and womanhood and the spirit of celebration.

II

In Portland, six houses—three men's houses and three women's houses—are connected with a neighborhood pentecostal church, the Maranatha Church. The pastor is black, the congregation nearly all white. That particular evening a municipal court judge, a negative, angry woman from Tacoma, was speaking. The crowd was a mixture of straights and hips, mostly white.

Afterwards, I inquired about a place for the night. I had my regular clothes on this time, a ruffled sport coat and blue trousers. Rick Probasco, who kindly arranged for me to stay at his House of Joy (not knowing I was a journalist) led me to think that I did not need to put on the old Salvation Army jeans to crash all the Jesus scenes. "Are you bumming through?" he asked, and I thought I was dressed for church!

On the way to the commune after church, Rick picked up a black hitchhiker. Jim (not really his name), the black, had a lot of weird responses, and it became obvious after a long and tortuous conversation that he had a mental history. Rick and I took him at face value for awhile. Then Jim would suddenly think one of us was laughing at him or was prejudiced. He would ask to get out of the car. Rick, the white, kept the discussion pretty much on Jesus. "I met Jesus as a person three-and-a-half years ago. Not a code or an ethic, and he opened up my mind to a new world, Jim."

Jim: "I already started, and I would like to be a better Christian."

Rick: "You can't go wrong on Jesus."

Jim: "You love me?"

Rick: "I sure do. Last thing I want to see is any harm come to you."

Jim: "You're lucky. No one knows I'm a Christian." He implied he was persecuted for being different in his beliefs in his black community. He switched to talk of "Africa, where everybody is safe," and to Rick, "I still fear you."

Rick invited him to come to the House of Joy sometime. We stopped so Jim could buy his mother a box of candy. I offered to buy a round of pop. Rick, the Jesus youth, didn't believe in such luxuries. Jim, the black, somehow was offended, as he had also been periodically by Rick's remarks. "You're laughing at me? That's the cruelest thing of all."

You can't carry on a conversation easily with a person who has such a complex. I just gave up, but Rick kept it up. His newfound black brother—deluded or not—was a brother for whom Christ died, and Rick, though perhaps unintentionally a bit patronizing, made it clear that Jim was welcome in his house any time.

At Renewal House in Los Angeles, a black sits in a stuffed chair, his white peers scattered around the room on a divan and on the floor. Black and white pray out loud, each several times. A white girl brings a black date to the Christian House for a Bible rap in Vacaville, Calif. A black fellow marries a white girl in the Children of God in Detroit. A black, Jesse Wise, walks with Arthur Blessitt in a 3,500-mile trek across the country from Los Angeles to Washington pushing a life-sized cross. Ann Walker, a black, heads a white commune (Fountain Chapel) in Vancouver, after splitting off from the Jesus People Army group. Blacks and whites discuss contemporary subjects in the Emmaus House, Toronto, and never think to mention race as a topic.

III

The coffee houses get a considerable mix, particularly those near university complexes. Take Agape House, for instance, initiated in a former newsstand by young Presbyterian and other laymen in northwest Washington, D.C., near Georgetown University. At Agape (the Greek term used in the New Testament for the highest form of love, usually translated as "charity" in the old King James version), Patty James, nineteen, a round-faced black with a natural hairdo, settled on the lap of Dan Hurkett, twenty-three, a clean-shaven, boyish-faced white boy who had left a coin exchange business to launch a men's fashion shop. The Agape store-front must surely be one of the more thoroughly integrated of Christian dwellings. In the table booths of the one-story building were people of every description, white, black, tripped out, straight; kids with hair so thick you couldn't even see their eyes, wearing sweat shirts, open shirts, coats and ties; a four-year old Oriental (daughter of an Agape helper) and skid-row bums, all enjoying the free food. Agape helps runaways and homeless youths in two communes. One is Don Alewood, nineteen, who drifted north after his parents were killed in a wreck and a brother was killed in Vietnam. The old men are not neglected, and the little parkway on a slope across the street is called after one drifter whom the youths dubbed "Freddie." Thus, "Freddie's Front Yard." Freddie slept in the park each night throughout the summer, but withstood pleas to be converted.

The theme of the Agape House ministry, according to Cary Habegger, twenty-two, soft-spoken graduate of Wheaton (Illinois) College, one of two full-time leaders, is Colossians 1:28, 29— which tells about preaching to every man "that we may present every man mature in Christ." The wide welcome at Agape is underscored by the one varied heap of jackets—plaid, leather, all types—piled in a corner beneath a poster of children, "Jesus loves all the little children." Scribbled on the wall is: "Smile—Jesus Loves You."

IV

Most houses seem open to blacks, although many, if not most, appear to be all white. Usually, the larger the house the more likely it will be to have some blacks. Houses having only six or seven persons usually report being all white. Areopagus, Inc., in Santa Barbara, California, reports nine black members, forty white; the Lighter Side of Darkness house in Springfield, Illinois, reports thirty members, four of them black; El Shadai House, Bellaire, Texas, and a coffee-house prayer meeting session run by John Struik in Rosedale, Ontario, are integrated but ratios are not indicated; the ten-member Love Inn, Freeville, New York, has one black. The Turning Point, Wailuku, Hawaii, is a coffee house with "no membership as such," but "welcomes persons of all ages, races and life styles."

One of the most impressively organized of all Jesus People efforts, Youth for Truth Outreach, Inc., Sacramento, is run by a black-led staff with 32 per cent of the fifty-four participants in the multi-phase program of communes and training being black. Another 7 per cent are Mexican-Americans and an additional 4 per cent are Latin Americans. Director of Youth for Truth is Harold Brinkley, twenty-nine, a black graduate of Fresno State College. Brinkley, who was in the Army for over three years, is a former counselor for the Sacramento County Juvenile Hall and former employment community worker for the Employment Youth Opportunity Center for California. Other staffers of Youth for Truth are Gene Browning, twenty-six, black, a former University of Texas halfback and a Methodist, as assistant director. Mrs. Tricia Gunner, white, twenty-five, of San Diego, is a girls' counselor; Robert Wright, black, twenty, a Baptist, attending Sacramento State College, is counselor for men and minister of music; Miss Frances Lackin, twenty-four, white, a Roman Catholic graduate of Salve Regina College in Newport, Rhode Island, from Massachusetts, is financial secretary; Miss Midge Henry, twenty, white, Roman Catholic background, is corresponding secretary.

Brinkley has no illusions as to what he is up against as a black in a white man's game. Because of a belief in the gifts of the Holy Spirit, he has to deal with the white pentecostal movement.

Many white pentecostals, as others, are accustomed to seeing their blacks as the focus of missionary work in Africa. Blacks have little use for the pentecostal movement in the United States, and denominations have little use for the independents, although Brinkley has gotten $1,200 from the Lutherans and $2,500 from the United Methodists. "Of course, we run into prejudice from the Assemblies of God churches," he says. "We try to go into churches, but there is a real fear there—maybe they feel some of our black fellows might date their white girls." He acknowledges that his staff, with the men black and the girls white, might stir such fears. And among the thirteen girls and nine fellows (six of the total are black) who live at Youth for Truth, several have long hair, "and they [pentecostals] are prejudiced against that." However, most of Brinkley's kids are neat and clean-shaven. "We believe that to attract attention to yourself is really a bummer. A Christian does not need a sign around his neck, but his attitude of change will speak for itself."

Brinkley is acquiring additional buildings in his balanced program. The complex includes a big three-story frame house with expansive divided basement, an outdoor patio with recreational facilities, two resident houses and hopefully a nearby gospel tabernacle which could be used for a chapel.

They get more than the gospel hearing. "A lot of houses have no program going," says Brinkley. "I feel they need some organization. There is a large group of people. People who say 'let the Lord do it' use it as an excuse. Their kids come and hang loose and spend the rest of their lives that way. We say get it together in six months or get out."

Sitting at a medium-sized desk in a modest office equipped with orderly files and two phones, an out basket, and fluorescent lighting, Brinkley outlined his two-part program. "The first three months we deal with their problems first and see how the Scripture is meaningful to them. Then in the second three months, we have a 're-entry' program. A lot come off the street with no job training. In order to go back as good Christian witnesses they need to go back as good citizens as well. We try to provide the skills." He said Christian businessmen are approached as individuals and as a group, but requests for jobs are usually ignored except for some talk and referrals to a board.

Brinkley keeps everybody working. Men are staining and shellacking the fence around the new cement patio. Beckey Elings, sixteen, white, of Sacramento, ironing in the basement, says, "I generally did not get along with my parents. I wanted to come here. Maybe I'll take something [of the faith] home. People here care."

While the center stays interracial, Brinkley wants particularly to get to the young black who grew up in the same hopeless type of ghetto he did in West Oakland, California. "I know the bitterness of the youth who feels trapped, who feels there is no opportunity, no way out for him. If he could only hear the truth about Jesus Christ, it could be the most liberating force in his life."

Brinkley is also active in organizing and attending meetings of Jesus People elders on the West Coast. Recently he sent letters to sixty houses on the West Coast for a joint meeting in Ventura (twenty-five responded). Such meetings could be the precursors to a larger organization or a federation, and men such as Brinkley could end up on top of a federation—if a federation could free itself of the institutional pastors and evangelists.

Blacks seem to be a real part of the movement. Whether or not the main-line church completely ignores them now is not really material to the blacks in the Jesus People movement. As they grow older, the blacks—and the whites of the Jesus People movement who continue working together without color hang-up—are likely to constitute the future church, in whatever form it takes. Certainly they are the church in their own estimation.

Integration is important to these youngsters. I remember auburn haired, Irish-smiling, green-eyed Doris Love, twenty, in long maxi dress in the kitchen of the Mansion Messiah, near Costa Mesa.

"The Lord told me to come here," she said. "I had come home from baby-sitting one night. My dad was mad. He had told me not to baby-sit for colored families, but I did. He was going to kick me out. So I left. He is not a Christian and is unhappy. Mother comes over here sometimes. The Lord speaks in a quiet way and gives real peace."

7

Jesus People Sex

Quietly at 2 A.M. in the morning, a dark-eyed young lady, working on cupcakes for a wedding the next day in the kitchen of a Jesus People commune, lets her hand slide along the top of the counter.

The elder of the commune in the Haight district of San Francisco has long since retired for the night.

The hand stops when it reaches another. The two do not look at each other, nor embrace. For there is still a matronly lady working on the intricate icing pattern of the wedding cake nearby.

Others, including two shabby guests who came knocking on the window at 1 A.M. for a place to sleep, are also nearby.

But the young lovers are relaxed enough for the young man, a singer in the commune's rock band, and the pensive, beautiful young lady in bathrobe to keep communications going.

In a world dedicated to the Spirit, there is still room for romance. Sometimes there is the temptation of the carnal. When five young men trying to live in the Spirit of the Lord in Phoenix, began to confess their sins, they found they all had the same "lust for Tina," a member of their Bible study group.

A Paw Paw, Michigan, joyful twenty-year-old girl in jeans and barefoot told of tickling the neighboring kids and ended up tickling the husky, former Karate expert now in her commune in Berkeley, California. "He's helpless and can't move. He's paralyzed when tickled," she laughed.

In a central California commune, Debbie Hall, twenty, rubs the leg of the elder, her fiance, a thin-faced youth, Robert Trusty, twenty-four, as he successfully concentrates on reading the Bible to his study group.

But normal boy-girl dating relations or even normal familial sister-brother relations are not always easy to establish in the young communes of Jesus People. The Jesus People communes—most of them run by peers no older than the other members—cover a variety of disciplines, all of them aimed at the Christian ideal. Many are outright puritanical, allowing no mixture of the sexes, except at mealtime or on street corners when evangelizing. Others allow dating, recognizing their members as mature adults. Others allow no dating or marriage plans without consent of the leaders.

If you are in the habit of crashing communes, you soon learn that Girls' House, House of Dawn, House of Rebekah, House of Ruth, and House of Esther, are girls' houses. And if you are a male, you're not going to sleep there that night. Or if you are female, you know that rules will bar you from the House of David, House of Joshua, etc. Nevertheless, most of the Jesus houses strive for a Christian fellowship of trust and family atmosphere.

I

Seated at dinner one quiet evening at Fisherman's Wharf in San Francisco, I talked with a young couple who had lived in Detroit's House of Prayer, the combination of old stores that had been made over into a big coffee house, commune, broadcast studio, and other facilities. Neither of the two young people was working. She was living with her mother and grandmother; he was sleeping in Golden Gate Park at night.

They were critical of the House of Prayer for many reasons, while testifying at the same time that the house did a lot of good getting kids off drugs and into less destructive and perhaps even positive trips. Among their reasons for criticizing: "We wanted to kiss," said Joey, nineteen, a blonde, baby-faced girl who loves her guitar and is sensitive to people. She said that she and her friend John, nineteen, at the House of Prayer would go off by themselves to the piano and steal a few kisses, and "We used to sneak downstairs and kiss at night."

One time, she said, they just wanted to talk. "We sneaked into the office and were rapping real heavy," but Brother George (George Bogle, Detroit-area Pentecostal minister who conducts radio programs and who organized the House of Prayer and its new counterpart in Pontiac), "wanted everybody asleep. He didn't want the neighbors to think we were swinging on the chandeliers."

But some goings-on would happen after dark. Both John and Joey said they knew of one couple at the House of Prayer who slipped down to the nursery room at night and had intercourse on the floor. Myrna Joy, twenty, now in Phoenix, who also lived at the House of Prayer, concurred. She said one couple—one of them a regular resident—had copulated at night in the nursery. But, she emphasized, any irregularity was far outshone by the good the house was doing. "No place is perfect," she said. "They did so much for me." She said members of the house had found her originally suffering from an overdose of drugs in a park, and they took her home.

Joey, in San Francisco, told of one boy in the Detroit House of Prayer who would sneak into the girls' dorm at night. John interrupted and said, "I practically killed him one night."

Joey continued, "I was sleeping. Then, suddenly, he [the intruder] was looking right in my eyes. I screamed and jumped like a rabbit."

In any group of people, you can find all types. In the Children of God commune in Los Angeles, as the commune warms up after midnight in celebration over new-found converts who are being brought in to testify while a rock band gives out with Jesus music and new improvised tunes, several girls kiss one another. Some of the girls also turn and kiss the boys, as a part of the after-midnight exuberance of dancing, singing and praising God. Later, one fellow who had stayed there a week told me some of the young men had been affectionate to one another, too. "They believe in greeting each other with a holy kiss," said Dennis, nineteen, now at the Berachah Farm at Petaluma, California. "The only ones I saw kissing at the Children of God center were two males. It was one distinct thing I remembered. And people were still up when I went to bed." Possibly the young ladies kissing one another were lesbians. It would not be unusual in a society of 250, on the basis of national figures, for 5 per cent to be homosexual.

Very few of the young ladies are sad-eyed, doleful or moping about with a spaced-out look. Their eyes—in most houses—sparkle as the radiant throne room of an enchanted land. Besides liberation of soul and spirit, there is a hint at times of Women's Lib. The girls often end up as chief cooks and bottle washers, a role some are chafing at. And this may in itself be one reason for splitting up the boys and girls into separate houses. The boys can then do their own cooking and dishwashing. Some of the messiest houses are the boy-girl houses.

But when the boys live by themselves, the house is run as immaculately as an old-fashioned monastery. A small cake pan with only a part of the cake left bothered Troy, the angelic-faced young man —singer and cook—whom we met at the House of Joy in Portland. He wanted to know who left it out on the clean table. Incidentally, that group had not lost all interest in the girls. They were in a bright mood at breakfast, for that day they were going over to do the lawn work at the Girls' House. One of the fellows was planning a wedding with one of the girls from that house, and the others joked about her being a better preacher than her husband-to-be.

The girls at Mansion Messiah, Costa Mesa, California, loved staying home and fixing the meals for the boys who have jobs and who go out witnessing. The boys are not allowed in the kitchen, unless helping.

At Berachah Farm, Petaluma, California, where a bunch of city slickers are trying to raise rabbits, goats and chickens, the elder, Ken Sanders, twenty, from Des Moines, allows a limited amount of dating. However, he wants the marriages to be between Christians, and he is about to crack down on one member who has been dating an "unsaved" girl in town.

"We're not a bunch of fundies," said Jean, a blonde in the Fellowship House, in Chicago, near Evanston, on Sheridan Road, just off the lake shore. She had broken her arm on the way to a leather shop where she worked, and the arm was now in a cast. Asked how long she had stayed out on a date, she said, "once all night," but explained that she had run into transportation problems. Usually a date might include an evening at the movies, then pizza and Coke at the commune. Apparently one of the most popular hours in this commune without many hang-ups is the Saturday night TV movie and pizza time—in the big commune basement of the building the neighbors used to call the haunted house. The house had been vacant much of the time, inhabited by gypsies once and once by a group of seminarians from Garrett Theological Seminary (Methodist) in Evanston, who, the rumor goes, turned it into a swinging wife-swapping commune. Now the Jesus People at their Fellowship House say, "Every Saturday night we watch Creature Feature," and with the pizza they eat as they watch the movie the youths admit to having a little wine or beer. Randy, who calls one of the more bossy girls "Mom," used to be down on girls—he thought they were all second class, his associates at Fellowship House say. But, it turns out, Randy had a series of car accidents, each time the other party in the accident being a girl. "It used to crack us up," his peers recall. Dating here, as in other Jesus People communes that allow outside dating, is kept pretty much among Christians. Dating others is to invite disharmony—bad vibes with the others and the risk of being asked to leave—they say. Randy was invited to leave the Fellowship House because he had become too fussy and negative, his peers said.

Romances are sometimes discouraged by allowing only one to be a member of a commune. Joey and John said they experienced this effort to split them up in Detroit and San Francisco. Don, nineteen, an ex-member of a British Columbia commune, said, "The chick I dug, they threw out. And then they said I was a rebellious spirit." He said the leader of the network of communes in the area doubled as a house father in a girls' commune. The wife of the leader was always insanely jealous, Don said. "There were fourteen chicks in the commune, and half were decent." The leader, however, never did chase the girls as the wife imagined, Don said. Also the wife saw to it that they had steaks and fine things while the leader's "shabby little doves" did without the finer things of life for Christ. Don said he walked out later when he was censured for planning to marry a girl from another commune. He was dressed with dapper tie and suit when I talked to him, calling himself "a step ahead," one step ahead of drug pushers, keeping clean while the police suspect him of involvement and try to pin a rap on him. He called the Jesus People leader further, "a money making bastard. I know he's making money . . . he is being walked all over (by his wife). When the last days come, I am willing to bet he will be scared of death . . . one of the first mistakes I made was to meet his wife . . . if I had been him, I'd taken one of the girls into the bedroom with his wife and ball the hell out of her." (I later talked to the leader Don described. He said: "Oh yes, Don's back in jail. I visited him last week.")

The houses, unless they are a part of a chain connected with a church or other concerns, are free to set their own rules. There comes the time when the men try to get rid of the more flighty or overprotective gal.

The half-dozen young men of Christian House, Vacaville, California, were ready to call it a night when a twenty-year-old chunky female, a recent convert, came over intent on finishing up her washing.

"I have to hang my clothes up," she insisted.

"God bless you Sheryl," one of the fellows said, looking up. "And keep you safe in every way tonight."

"Can I finish what I was going to say?" she said.

"What's another five minutes when she's had twenty-five already?"

"Live by the spirit and not the letter," she said.

"God rest you, Sheryl," one said, and she began to leave, disgruntled.

And another added, "And may you see visions!"

II

I would say the sexual life of the Jesus youth is fairly normal, at least by middle-class standards. The middle-class church code expects chastity, celibacy of the nonmarried, and fidelity in marriage. The Jesus People try to put down sex, pretending it is not very important, when Jesus is all. There are exceptions, as we have noted, and they often talk the language of ordinary youth, as their humor indicates (Paula, a sweet, beautiful young lady who split from a drug farm and her husband because she was hungry, found her way to town and was converted, answers the phone by the table at suppertime in Smyrna House, Toronto: "Male or female?" The answer is "Male." She responds, "Praise the Lord!"). The fires of romance burn even as they did in Victorian novels. Some may be getting married young, like Diane Branton and Brian MacLaren, at Smyrna House. She is sixteen; he is seventeen.

The members of the wedding sometimes are in tuxedos and bridal gowns, as planned in Portland; or dressed in sackcloth, reading Scripture and drinking wine, as at a ceremony of the Children of God—"the weirdest marriage I have ever seen," recalls Mrs. Peggy Justus. Often the scene is outdoors, and Golden Gate Park in San Francisco has seen its share. Or consider the wedding of Reggie Burton, twenty-one, and Sue McNichol, twenty, near Vacaville, California. Bizarre but traditional, and certainly filled with sanctity, the wedding performed by a licensed minister took place on a sloping pasture, by a clear, rippling creek. There were three circles of flowers—one for Reggie, one for Sue, and one for the minister.

There was talk about the miracles of life and of the sky at that wedding. A cow settled down behind the flower rings and gave birth to a calf just fifteen minutes before the ceremony, and looked on with her freshly born offspring. People dotted the hillside of the farm where the fences had been taken down. "The clouds parted," said Dan Hardesty, nineteen, a former Catholic seminarian, now at the Christian House, Vacaville. "There was a blue *J* formed in the clear blue that showed through the clouds." He and others took the semblance to *J*, of course, as standing for Jesus.

The wedding was followed with a reception in a park with ten gallons of spaghetti, cakes, Jell-O, salads. Reggie pushed a piece of wedding cake playfully into Sue's face. The bride, in her old-fashioned high necked dress, responded by grinding a piece of cake into the face of the groom, who wore an open shirt and striped beige and brown pants. There was laughter. It all seemed a miracle.

The Jesus People are fairly bourgeois (if not actually puritanical) in their sexual ethic, like their parents in city and suburbia. Perhaps some of the same criticism applied to the confused, stifled parents of the nuclear family by Cox and others could be applied to some of the righteous Jesus People. Sex cannot be overlooked or put down. "Sex and religion are the two most powerful non-rational forces of the human personality," says Andrew Greeley, of the National Opinion Research Center of the Center for the Study of American

Pluralism, University of Chicago. "That they should be linked, and even allied in their battle to overthrow the tyranny of reason, is surprising only to the highly Jansenized Christian [Cornelius Jansen, bishop who lived 1585 to 1639, in Ypres, Belgium, believed in the total depravity of man and that only those predestined in advance will be saved] who has lost sight of the sexual imagery in his own faith—the intercourse, or the pervasive comparisons of the Church to marriage in both the Old and New Testament." [1]

Among those in communes who say they remain celibate and even asexual, there may emerge some serious difficulties, although the average commune provides a healthy counterbalance with its familial atmosphere. But some who prefer to ignore sex may be building a base for frustrations that could emerge and shape their lives unhappily in the future. The puritanical types among the Jesus People of today could become a generation's frustrated dirty old men of tomorrow. If they remain religious, and if they find later in a non-isolated, non-rural society that their frustrations must eventually be channeled, they could lead religion into and beyond the new morality into licentiousness and an overemphasis on sex.

The Jesus People will have to be careful they are not, for all of their righteousness and talk of sexual purity, sowing the seeds for the time when they hit age thirty-five, forty, or forty-five and then look back in panic and move into a less conscious, less manageable world of sexual pursuits. "Reason cannot rule over the passions and emotions of man as a tyrant, at least not for very long," says Greeley, "without running the risk of having an open revolution on its hands. Religion has always been conscious, implicitly that man is more than mind—that he is also 'soma' and "pneuma'—that is to say, both body and spirit—and that while these two characteristics of human personality seem to be opposed to each other in theory, in fact, they are quite closely related and frequently in alliance against prosaic, secular, everyday rationality." [2]

Fortunately for those who marry from the Jesus communities, they usually return to that community at least pro tem, and their marriage escapes the packaged, materialistic look of affluence-seeking American families caught in their isolated compartments and nonsocietal pursuits. Also on the plus side of the sexual dilemma, some of the communes possibly provide the celebrative aspect and the joy that marriage needs to achieve its fullest meaning.

III

In their more personal moments, how do the Jesus People talk about sex among themselves? Talk about it they do, as we have seen, and I suppose to an analyst this "talking" and "talk-out" is healthy. Again, even here, the thoughts of the Jesus People are framed in Scriptural precepts. But they are thinking, and sex is not dead. Perhaps there is no better way to find out where the Jesus People really are—at least some of them—than to listen in on a bunch of young men in a talk session late at night.

At Emmaus House, Toronto, the young men, now in their bunks for the night, with only one night light burning, after a young lady (just married) who had talked to them in the doorway for awhile was gone, turn to marriage and sex.

"I think it was that way from the beginning—one flesh," said one.

"I agree with that," said another, "but I see a plan set up by God —people were balling all the time in Abraham's day. God toned it down to one wife."

"I see it all as an example for us. Paul said all Scripture is given for our benefit—see, it came down to two."

They continued to struggle for an answer to the fact that God allowed polygamy through much of the Old Testament.

"God wanted us to see what they went through for our benefit."

"They were waiting around for the great marriage."

"Amen."

"If the Lord did not reveal this to us, we would say 'I wonder why.' "

"You can't figure God out."

"I'm glad I can't."

"Praise the Lord—He then wouldn't be God."

The discussion moved on to acquaintances at school and then one mentioned "John the beloved" in the Bible—"Jesus' best friend."

"They didn't like him (after Jesus' death) for he was still hangin' around with other freaks."

"They tried to boil him in oil somewhere, and he wouldn't die."

"There was still something for him to do."

"Like Revelation—writing it."

"I Corinthians 13—Love is so important."

"With love comes suffering."

"Suffering?"

"Yes—there's been this verse over my head, that God would make you suffer—'In the world ye shall have tribulation; but be of good cheer, I have overcome the world' " (Jn. 16:35).

"Far-out."

They began to tire, and well they might—it was well after midnight. The plan was for all to get up early so as to get seats at a Kathryn Kuhlman rally a half mile away in a civic stadium.

"Sweet dreams of Jesus," one of the young men said, and others repeated the phrase. Another, "Amen," and so to sleep.

In Milwaukee, at Sheepfold House, as the youths wake up and head for the bathroom, they are immediately reminded of love for Jesus in vernacular terms.

The graffiti just behind the bathroom door, in evidence as you close it, has the letters of Jesus' name: "JESUS" is across the top, with "Jesus" also spelled down from the first "J," "Saves" from the first "S," and "Souls" down from the last letter. Written around it are: "Pant, pant, pant." There is a drawing of a heart. "Smack . . . my hero."—all referring to Jesus as their first love.

At least they haven't forgotten what life is all about—love. And they retain the popular vocabulary of romance and of attraction. They retain their own identity and expression. These Jesus youths are struggling for meaning in personal relations just as the rest of society is. And, despite their cliches and outward exclamations, they may, with their commune experience and interpersonal trips thrown in, indeed have something to contribute to developing a healthier sexual climate in the United States.

8

Links With the Occult

"The toilet didn't work, so she rebuked the demons out of the toilet in the name of Jesus. I remember laughing about it. They are on a witch-hunt all the time."

The young man, now in San Francisco, was describing life in the House of Prayer in Detroit.

The Jesus movement does have some strange similarities to the occult. First of all, Jesus People believe in many of the same things that occultists believe in, and in some cases, particularly in regard to the existence of extraterrestrial possessive beings, with more clarity.

The Jesus People, in their deep interpersonal relations with one another—and God—deal with real and/or imagined beings in the universe. Sometimes they sound like a rerun of the Dark Ages, with evil beings hovering around like gargoyles atop a Gothic cathedral.

Consider what they say about the Devil:

—Carlos Alonso, El Shaddai House, Bellaire, Texas: "We have no problems. The devils and demons do."

—Pat Boone, singer: "The Devil is fighting tooth and toenail. He sees what is happening, as it was in the first century, as this movement picks up steam. Thousands, maybe millions (coming to Jesus). The Devil sees his time shortened. The Devil is pouring out his unholy spirit on earth—e.g., drugs, the occult, movies of witches and bloodletting."

—Craig Skinner, twenty-six, caretaker at a deserted Jesus People camp at Garland Hot Springs, Washington: "I came to a point where I had a definite choice—Satan and die or the Lord and live.

I was awakened one night at three A.M. Something came in human form, floating in. I was like mesmerized . . . a tight feeling . . . a whirling sensation . . . pressure . . . the thing came over next to me and knelt down. It had an iridescent smile. A spirit, but not one of the Lord's—apparently—it jumped in me as I blacked out. Satan made me feel I would die that night. I was possessed . . . terrified. Rockets attacking and blowing up are not as scary or as deep as this terror. I told the people at the house to call the morgue. I went to different people for help . . . these brothers on the floor. I had no strength . . . I regained strength and lay down. Satan came on again. The depression came back. I told a girl to light a candle and hold my hand. The oppression and depression were heavy. I felt my body withering, drying up and blowing away. A sense of a skeleton and skin blowing away. 'I got to have a Bible. . . .' As soon as I said that, I felt like a wind washed down and over my body and all that. Oppression was gone. My body felt still. A soothing, cooling wind made me whole."

I

Exorcism—the rite of casting out devils and demons—is a part of many Jesus People services, particularly the larger ones with pentecostal ties. The House of Prayer, under Jack Williams in Pontiac, calls on God to bring out the demons at every service. And one Assemblies of God couple in Pontiac regularly casts out demons from young Jesus People and their friends in their home.

Mr. and Mrs. Robert Cornforth report that they have cast out demons from some seventy youths. Several nights a week you might find a boy friend bringing a girl friend, or vice versa, for the demon-casting-out effort. The Cornforths have taped a half dozen demon-casting-out sessions in their Spanish-décor brick Waterford Township home near Pontiac.

"I know it sounds weird," says Mrs. Cornforth, "but it's all in the Bible. Jesus does it." On the basis of such events in the life of Jesus (cf. Mk. 1:34; 3:15; 7:29; 9:38, etc.), the Cornforths believe their efforts are diametrically opposed to the occult rather than being a part of it.

Actually the idea is not limited to holiness and pentecostal churches. Most religious traditions have some practice—present or past—for the exorcism of demons. Roman Catholics, Eastern Orthodox, and Episcopalians still have prayers for casting out demons in their regular church rites, particularly at baptism, and the prayers are said only by the priest. "Do you renounce evil and Satan and all his representatives and all his wisdom and all that represents evil?" a Greek Orthodox priest asks a godfather at a baptism. "Exorcism" means literally from the Greek "to bind with an oath." The use of holy names, the early Christians argued, distinguished the practice from magic.

The Cornforths' demon-casting style contrasts with others. Many who exorcise demons, especially faith healers who bring out demons from a person, leave that person emotionally wracked and silent. The Cornforths' tapes show a lively dialogue between the "possessed" youth and the other kids and adults. The exorcists are laughing, shouting, giving ultimatums to the "demons." It's the voice —usually heavy and drab—of the youth possessed that is heard and interpreted as the voice of demons. The youth argues with the exorcists.

The tapes go like this:

YOUTHS AND CORNFORTH: "Come out in the name of Jesus. What is your name?"

SHANE (his voice is interpreted as that of the demon in control of him): "Black cat."

YOUTHS ET AL.: "Well, come out."

SHANE: "I am more."

YOUTHS: "How many?"

SHANE: "Six thousand."

YOUTHS: "Come out; you got five minutes."

(They prattle in tongues—strange syllables—as they pray in the name of the Holy Spirit of God against the demons.)

YOUTHS: "The blood of Jesus covers you. How long you been in there, black cat?"

SHANE: "A long time."

YOUTHS: "How many years?"

SHANE: "Two years."

(The youths laugh, ridiculing the demon.)

YOUTHS: "Come on out."

(Shane is groaning and heaving.)

(Mrs. Cornforth stops the tapes and says: "Hear the noises he's making. The spirit is coming out.")

YOUTHS: "Come on out. You got thirty seconds now to get out to the pit. Get out! Out!"

Another, David, sat barefoot with his arm around his girl friend and told of his life with demons and his freedom now. He was first possessed in an Evansville, Indiana, zoo "looking through a glass at snakes. I felt something come over my eyes." Deliverance for the seventeen-year-old, who hopes to return to high school, came at the Cornforths', but he said later the same demons returned, woke him up, turned on lights and harassed him.

The Cornforths are critical of spiritualism and seances and believe any alleged talking with the dead is talking only to demons. There is no reincarnation but a reincarnation of demons, which might help one to recollect previous existences of the demons in other bodies, said Mrs. Cornforth.

A main-line church reaction was expressed by the Rev. John Pipe, director of education for the Detroit Association of American Baptist Churches. He said, "My feeling is that the people who believed in demons in Biblical times would have doubts about them if these people lived today." He said Jesus referred to demons "because he was a product of his day. This was his way of expressing the evil or negative or anti-human side of existence. My feeling is that the current emphasis on demons in some groups is a going back to old superstition and witchcraft."

Dr. Charles Solley, professor of psychology, Wayne State University, Detroit, said that the demon activity enunciated among the Jesus People by the Cornforths and others "may exist because man is still a very superstitious character. He is afraid of the unknown." Dr. Solley said demon-consciousness can also be the result of "the power of suggestion" and "can even be a form of self-hypnosis."

II

You can wonder who is the more real and who is really God— God or the Devil. To which one should a person pay the most attention—running from the Devil, thus negatively taking directions from him, or serving God affirmatively, and the Devil be damned? Whatever it means, the Jesus People think a lot of—or rather, about—devils and the Devil. Of all the harsh things said about the Jesus People by armchair critics—about psychological hang-ups and frustrations and being victims of an anticultural and antiestablishment spirit rather than being for something—one harsh question that is not usually asked could be considered: *Are they in reality worshiping the Devil?*

Consider what worship is. It is first of all a recognition of the reality of an object. Secondly, it is then ascribing some homage or subservience or response to that object (or Person), specifically to placate or make that object happy. Oh, yes, worship is also thanksgiving. But how much actual worship is thanksgiving? In the pews on Sunday, the spirit of the prayers, if not the words, is the placating of an angry God—thanking him maybe, in that he overlooked Aunt Jane by not calling her home, or thanking him for good health, a sort of finger crossing. One is thankful in worship that all the wickedness and potential evil and bad health have been escaped. I have long contended, by observing different churches, faiths and cults at worship, that you could substitute the name of God in Sunday morning worship with the name of the Devil and it wouldn't make a "hell" of a lot of difference. The Jesus People most certainly spend a lot of time talking about the Devil—and to him—as they exorcise his emissaries even from the crockery. To the extent that their lives are patterned around consciousness of the Devil, you could argue that they worship him. Listening to—and following, even in reaction—a particular objective entity, here or out there, is worshiping.

Curiously, this extreme consciousness of the Devil and of "principalities" (Rom. 8:38) that so easily surround us is itself a mark distinguishing the Jesus People from the Devil and satanic-minded cults. I spent an afternoon in San Francisco with Anton LaVey, the bald, smiling former lion tamer and police photographer with a Fu Manchu mustache who heads the Satan cult in the U.S. out of his black house with painted-over windows near Golden Gate park. To my surprise, he did not believe in an objective Satan. For him it is a concept for helping to release man from his guilt complexes and to allow him to adopt a hedonistic philosophy of life.

The Jesus People, then, go beyond the Devil worshipers in their Devil worship. The Devil (or Satan) is real to them. But again, this does not distinguish the Jesus People. The Jesus People are assimilating a concept of Protestant fundamentalism—Devil worship, an all-compelling consciousness of the existence of a real demonic force, with legions of cohorts, and an awareness that demands special attention.

While main-line Protestants talk of the Devil and his cohorts in their prayers, the Jesus People talk of them every day. At first glance, this could be ascribed to a new medievalism and a new supersition. Father Greeley says of the Jesus People and demons, "I suppose it's an attempt to explain evil in the world." It is possible also to argue—in the light of the interpersonal life of the commune and the commitment of the Jesus People to a Person—that demon consciousness is a part of an intense and healthy personalism that refuses to deal with people as forces or as inanimate.

III

The fact that the Jesus People border on various facets of the occult is really not too unusual. The history of the church has its share of superstitions, customs, fears and the paranormal (Lourdes, Fatima, Czestochowa, etc.). Every Catholic knows of the excesses of Mariology, and of the veneration of bones and other objects. Protestants live by the superstition of conformity. Many have a magical belief in the efficacy of being at church at a certain time, keeping a regular practice, carrying a Bible, holding to a magical number, such as seven for the day of worship or ten, for the approved amount in giving or three in the magic formulas invoking the Trinity for special power at the end of prayers, and even One— the most mystical number of all, for Christians, Jews and Moslems.

The Jesus People place less store in numbers than their seniors. The cultish Children of God, as has been pointed out, were up all night at their main building in Los Angeles, reveling in praise and dancing, and slept nearly all day Sunday. Others, like the oft-moving commune run by Ralph Morrison in Detroit, schedule a

Bible study at four P.M. on Sunday afternoon, one of a chain of Bible studies each day. Some, particularly those communes that exist around church hucksters and big Bible preachers, get their young followers to toe to an 11 A.M. worship service to a degree. But Jesus People don't follow in step too well on the seventh-day concept. If they have a hang-up on numbers, it is the hang-up Jesus had about numbers—the seeking of the one lost sheep and counting him with vigor and ceremony when he comes into the fold for the Lord.

Despite a vital interest in prophecy, the new Jesus youths appear to say little about numbers. Hal Lindsey, of the J. C. Light and Power Co., the fairly straight, almost Campus Crusade type of movement, with its clean-cut athletes and fraternity-type members, dwells on the number bit in his popular book on prophecy, *The Late Great Planet Earth.* Says Lindsey about the last days: "Everyone will be given a tattoo or mark on either his forehead or forehand, only if he swears allegiance to the Dictator as being God. Symbolically, this mark will be 666. Six is said to be the number of man in Scripture and a triad or three is the number for God. Consequently, when you triple 'six' it is the symbol of man making himself God." [1]

However, I don't remember hearing any Jesus youths themselves talk about 666 representing the Devil, or 144,000 the number saved (Rev. 14:3), etc. The numbers game they leave to I Ching and the tarot card cult and to the 11 A.M. observing, tithing senior Christians and those who come in with the old-style fundamentalist numbers game (Lindsey is a graduate of Dallas Theological Seminary).

The real message of Satan and demon consciousness among the Jesus youth is not simply the fact of occult overtones. The real significance is in the negativism inherent in such Jesus People occult concepts. The Jesus People are saying they reject the present culture, the present establishment, and most of all the present church. The occult syndrome underscores the negativism in the movement —what they are against. When and if the movement begins to turn, as it probably will, toward sentimentality, if for no other reason than the process of aging, its members may begin to regard the forces "out there" as more beneficent. Even as they study the Bible and show a more complete concept—and they are open to Scripture —they will realize that the Bible talks about "nice" extraterrestrial visitors to earth, who appeared to people like Abraham, Gideon, Mary, Paul, the disciples at the tomb and on the Mount. When this positivism in subject matter emerges, if it does, then the movement could evolve toward a spiritualism (and séances) or more substantially to a social consciousness in terms of greater responsibility, much as traditional Catholic devotion to the saints has pictured them looking over their shoulders inspiring them to good works. The new saints have yet to discover the old saints and to articulate an understanding of the characteristics of sainthood. They have not listened to Hebrews 12:1: "Therefore, since we are surrounded by so great a cloud of witnesses [the saints]. . . ."

IV

What are some of the other parallels—beyond demons and extraterrestrial personalities—that link the Jesus People with the occult? What does further identity with the occult mean?

The occult also embraces the mysterious, the unknown, the nondefinable. Again, there is similarity to other expressions of faith. In all religions there is a mystical quality. "The fact is, of course, that Christianity and Judaism are also Eastern religions," says Dr. Gabriel Fackre, professor of theology at Andover Newton Theological School, who studied Eastern religions recently while a visiting professor at the University of Hawaii. "As such, they are sensitive to the dimensions of mystery and unity that draw the counterculture to other Eastern options. Eastern Orthodox explore the mystical depths. St. Francis celebrates the living earth of the ecologists, and Christian history records numberless communitarian experiments. And Judaism has counterparts to these." [2]

The Jesus People help to set up or rediscover this rapport of Christianity with the mystical bent of the East. Says Dr. Martin Marty, professor of modern church history, University of Chicago:

I have predicted for some time that the Eastern religious styles popular in youth culture would influence the West but would not prevail here; eventually, they would transfuse and transform the Western religious tradition rather than replace it. And that is to the good, I would think. The Christian World Liberation Front and other street-people Christians are signs that the moment is here. A couple of years ago, during the neo-religious kick, any superstition, magical or mystical experience, or religious tenet was respectable on a campus or in a commune—any that is, except if associated with the West's historic faith. Now, in effect, the freaks are saying that our culture 'can go home again' with a somewhat altered style of consciousness. In their own way, they offer another mode of witness to that tradition.[3]

Among Christian occult books is the nineteenth century *Aquarian Gospel of Jesus the Christ*[4] by Levi H. Dowling, son of a Disciples of Christ frontier preacher. The Aquarian Gospel supplies details in the silent years of Christ's early life, purportedly given to Levi in early morning visions in the "Akashic Records," the "imperishable records of life" which are in the Universal Mind and whose reader must be in such close touch with the spirit of the Supreme Intelligence, according to an introduction to the book by a relative, "that every thought vibration is instantly felt in every fibre of his being."[5] This "Gospel" covers Christ's missing life, according to Levi, in Tibet, Greece and Egypt. And there are the lost Gospels of Thomas, spurious but ancient tracts, discovered in Egypt.

"The Jesus People are a part of it all (the occult revival)," says Stephen Erlewine, manager of Circle Books, biggest occult book dealer in the Detroit area, in Ann Arbor. "The Jesus People are spiritually involved. The occult means simply 'hidden.' The Jesus People are dealing with the hidden nature of man. Anything that approaches some spiritual understanding is occult." He says some of the people who were on to magic moved on to the Jesus People, although I found by and large that the Jesus People were not heavy into magic even though they might have been heavy into drugs. (One of the exceptions is the elder of the House of Emmaus, Toronto, Robert Velick, a former Roman Catholic born in Yugoslavia. He once wrote a magic column for an underground newspaper and has kept Wu as his nickname because it stands for "nothingness" in Taoist philosophy. He notes that when he came to Christ, Christ did not lead him to change his name.) Erlewine adds: "Some have moved the other way, too," from the Jesus People into magic. "Obviously it (the Jesus movement) didn't work for them

personally." Why? "If there is any distinction occultism might have
with other systems, it leaves some room for emphasis on the individual." Erlewine also said there is more room for positive thinking
in the occult. But he does not believe it offers any greater
truths. "No, you reach the same understanding either way. Some
Jesus freaks become well integrated (in personality), but some
don't. Some are self crusaders and lose a breadth of understanding.
And this is not what Christ meant." Erlewine also noted the great
difficulty youths have coming into the occult—there is so much to
learn, terminology, techniques, etc. One can argue that the Jesus
People offer a more simplistic approach to the occult—there are
immediate results. But again, the Jesus People demand much Bible
study, and they are probing into commentaries and various Bible
translations, with a real yen for study. Thus perhaps both sides of
the occult—the Christian and the non-Christian—provide a challenge for the imaginative, inquisitive minds of the young as they are
concerned with the future things more than with the study of science
and other practical day-by-day courses of a college curriculum.

It is easy for American Christians to be alarmed over the increase of the occult. The media do much to promote the subject, for
heaven knows it is colorful reading. Even the Catholic press has
taken it up. The *Catholic Weekly* diocesan paper in the Lansing
(Michigan) Diocese (Aug. 13, 1971) put this headline over a
Religious News Service story on the occult. "The 'Occult' Explosion
Rocks the United States" with a top-line of "Devil worship, astrology, voodoo, ouija boards, I Ching." And the RNS statistics whetted
the appetite (and prejudices) and concern over the increase of evil
and evil things. For example: There are now an estimated 400
witch covens in the U.S.; Jeane Dixon's *A Gift of Prophecy* has sold
over 3 million copies; 40 million Americans seek guidance from
10,000 astrologers in a $200-million-a-year business; spiritualism
is reviving, there being now an estimated 150,000 members in 400
churches; high schools and even universities, such as the University
of South Carolina, New York University, and the University of Alabama offer courses in the history of witchcraft, magic and sorcery.
Book clubs have recently asked for 400,000 more copies of *Linda
Goodman's Sun Signs,* of which Taplinger has sold more than 262,-
000, according to *Publishers' Weekly,* August 23, 1971.

The commune by definition appears to imply supernatural occult concerns, according to Dr. Stanley Krippner of the Maimonides Medical Center, Brooklyn. He reported a first hand study of twenty-two communes with an epiphenomenal equality running through most of them. Reporting to the Society for the Scientific Study of Religion, Dr. Krippner said of the study: "The experiences reported range from telepathy to clairvoyance to prophecy to reincarnation. Whether or not the events occurred, it is remarkable that belief in the paranormal is virtually an act of faith held by communal inhabitants—not questioned as it would be in many sections of 'straight' society." [6] His selections ranged from the Now House in California in a forest near an old Indian meeting ground—the leader in the non-drug commune claimed to have direct communication with Christ—to the New Buffalo commune in New Mexico where members used tarot cards to determine the future and the ouija board to communicate with spiritual beings.

The Jesus People contribute to an interest in the occult in many ways: (1) In their more cultic or secret forms they encourage such things as private covens; (2) The easy Jesus People formulas, even the often heard "Praise God," have a sound of the magic as they are used to shore up feelings or dispel problems; (3) The Jesus People have an other worldly concern with spirits, demons; (4) They lean to more ghostly topics and prophecies, such as Daniel, Ezekiel, and Revelation, as they form a suspenseful occult mood; (5) The Devil is as real as God; (6) The Jesus People with their demonology and all are contributing to the language of the occult; (7) They even accent much of the middle America rural *Farmer's Almanac* type of superstition, *e.g.*, as they carry objects (Bibles) and say some words (prayer) before each act, as the kids in Ellenville, New York, do when they pray as they get in and out of cars.

Does the steady hand of middle-class culture stay many who come out of Presbyterian, Baptist, Roman Catholic, or Jewish homes? Another factor probably mitigating against direct involvement in Eastern terminology by the Jesus People is the fact that their roots are in an experience identified with Jesus, who has been presented through the medium of Western customs and language. Hence, they feel more at home with the vocabulary that has traditionally surrounded Jesus and certainly with the vocabulary of the Scriptures that tell of Jesus.

Yet the dichotomy is due to more than just language. It is rooted in the very nature of Christianity. The oriental mystic peers of the Jesus People are hard on them. I asked some yoga-consciousness kids in an Integral Yoga Institute class to tell me what they thought of the Jesus People. Said Peggi, a former Roman Catholic with twelve years in Catholic schools, "Jesus freaks are remnants of the Piscian age. They are clinging to concepts of separation and darkness. Yoga is union and the light of knowledge. It is universal and positive and in direct opposition to those who teach of a God who can condemn eternally those he created in love, which is illogical, inconsistent and just plain ignorant. I met up with some folks from the Berean Christian Fellowship in Dallas who say that if you sin long enough God will 'turn his face from you and you'll be damned.' Hogwash!" Donna, a former Methodist and now a Unitarian-Universalist, into yoga and Zen, said: "I have received literature from these [Jesus] people. Although they were very straight-looking, their literature was geared to freaky people. Frankly I was turned off and mad at them for using the hip culture to expound the dead gospel which I myself had been reared in. It is really absurd of them to try to lure people back to this ridiculous Christian belief which has been so bigoted, conservative in the past."

V

There are a number of thriving new youth groups that look to Jesus that I would label overt (non-subtle) occult Jesus People groups.

FIRST, I would include the Children of God Jesus People because of their explicit belief in the magic of words, their exclusiveness of style and the utter secrecy with which they surround themselves. Try to get the real name of one of the members, as we have noted, and you get "Joshua," "Apollos," etc., because all that counts is God and Jesus. There is the mystical blindness—one path or nothing. And only they can interpret it. They seek only a repetition of a formula that says "Jesus saved me." Nothing else is expected except to serve the Lord in that locale, which means only, and I emphasize *only*, going out into the highways and byways and reciting almost hypnotically a few texts (they must learn two a day) from sets of verses. There is little essential difference between these youths and the Hare Krishna cult of young people, although the Children of God do not shave their heads and they utilize a different vocabulary. The chief guru of the Kundalini yoga movement, with its sixty centers in the U.S., commented on the similar hard, simplistic occult style of the Hare Krishna and Jesus People cultists in an interview over lunch in a nature food restaurant. Swami Bhajan said, "The Hare Krishna say they are the only way. The Jesus People say they are. If Jesus is the only way, they all mess up the whole thing. For Jesus is everybody's way." Christ consciousness was a valid concept for him: "You have to be in perfect yoga—detach self, live in high consciousness, above every element. I agree. He [Jesus] was the only way—but *be* as he was—this does not mean do weird things. There is too much monkeying of simple language. If you love him, be like him."

The Children of God are more occult than the occult—more so than the Church of Satan, which receives visitors and answers questions (although banning the public from rites), and more occult than a spiritualist séance, for a séance seeks at least to reveal; the Children of God seek to conceal and play games, giving only minimal information; they always make you think you are missing something, even if it is only their own identity.

SECOND, among overt Jesus People occult groups you must consider the enigmatic Church in Los Angeles. Known outside Los Angeles as "the Local Church," or the "Local Church in Toronto," in "Cleveland," depending on where they are meeting, the group recognizes only one church in each locality. Although made up mostly of straights—about one-third middle-class Chinese at the Los Angeles mother church (founded by two Chinese evangelists, Watchman Nee and Witness Lee, who originally worked in Foochow and Shanghai)—and denouncing any connection or even interest in the Jesus People, this movement has been assimilated and copied nevertheless by the Jesus People.

It was in Phoenix that I first became aware of the influence of Nee and Lee. There, barefoot and bearded Harry Rogers, twenty-three, was conducting a shouting Bible-study session with books and pamphlets by Nee and Lee. The Children of God and some Northwest houses, such as the House of Joy in Portland, follow a similar style. One will often find Nee's and Lee's books on tables of Jesus People literature at rallies.

The anti-institutionalism and anti-church attitudes of Nee and Lee are believed, also, to have influenced the concepts of Berg and the Children of God directly. While acknowledging no doctrine, "the Local Church" movement nevertheless has its own acceptable concepts. "In principle, we practice events according to the teaching of the Bible," Lee told me in an interview. These practices include baptism by immersion, communion, and, for the leaders, footwashing.

The real name of Witness Lee, sixty-five, is Lee Chang Shou. He is the direct link to founder Watchman Nee, originally Nee To-sheng, who established the first "Local Church" in 1922 in his native Foochow. Lee came into contact with Nee in 1926 in Shanghai.

The typical Local Church rite is centered on a list of a dozen Bible verses on a blackboard. They are shouted out by individuals, and the phrases are reaffirmed over and over again. At one meeting, as groups got up and shouted out together, one of the more freakish members, Barbara James, twenty-one, from Akron, grabbed my arm and said, "Now let's read that together!" but I passed up the dual recitation.

Critics note that despite its claim of being all inclusive, biblically based and nondenominational, the Local Church is a tight little clique, as well as noisy. Mrs. William Eichmeyer and son Kurt, of Phoenix, told me of having the Phoenix Local Church group at a session of Jesus People who hold regular Saturday night sessions in their spacious, carpeted living room. "They think they are the only church," Mrs. Eichmeyer said. "They come here and overcome all by shouting. Everything that is said gets an 'Amen,' and if you magnify that by seventy kids here, it's deafening."

The use of the Chinese-oriented Church in Los Angeles style, derived as it was on the China mainland, perhaps influenced by the free-style all-speak-up Chinese school classroom, points up in another way the debt of the Jesus People to the religions of the East, particularly the more occult types that demand both secrecy and constantly ascending new highs of enthusiasm. (Curiously, there was a Jesus Movement in the early days of Communist China. Its communal approach was a threat to the Communists and the movement was eventually crushed. It is recounted in *The "Jesus Family" in Communist China,* by Dr. D. Vaughan Rees.

THIRD, among the more obvious occult-oriented fringe movements that could be considered a part of the new Jesus youth scene is The Way Biblical Research Center in New Knoxville, Ohio. Founder Victor P. Wierville, fifty-four, with headquarters in New Knoxville, bases his movement on ancient Christian heresies, Christian Science and Unity thought and a pious humanism. Jesus is not God and there is no Trinity, Wierville believes. And he divides up Scripture much like Marcion, second century Gnostic, who rejected the Old Testament for Christians. Likewise, Wierville insists that the Old Testament is for the Jews and the Gospels for Christians. Right belief, he says, will protect Christians from harm even in war. Joined by Steve Heefner, once with the original House of Acts, Novato, Calif. Wierville, a former Evangelical and Reformed clergyman who studied at Princeton and the University of Chicago, specializes in courses on tapes and film.

FOURTH, on the street corners in Chicago, Toronto and other cities, there are representatives, dressed in somber black and grey robes, sinister as the Devil, of the Process Church of the Final Judgment. The group began in London in 1963 with Robert De-Grimston, with emphasis more on psychology than religion.

In 1967, the movement came to New Orleans and San Francisco. DeGrimston, a former Anglican, a young man, is the main teacher and moves about among his followers instructing them. The followers are indeed grim as they wear three-horned goat head symbols and silver crosses. Their message, like that of the Church of Satan, appears to be more a self-realization or self-betterment philosophy than metaphysics. But they do recognize three great gods of the universe. These are Jehovah, "a god of vengeance and retribution," who inspires discipline and courage; Lucifer, not to be confused with Satan, the bringer of light who also urges a life of enjoyment, gentleness and kindness; and Satan, who brings out the worst in man, hurling him toward corruption and depravity on the one hand and beyond to human achievement and self-sacrifice on the other hand. To this group, Christ becomes a unifier whose mission is to reconcile the three different gods in conflict. Salvation results from the reconciliation of opposites. That is, if one tends to be more Luciferian he must try to achieve more of the qualities of Jehovah and Satan, and so on. Members look to an impending end of the world, which will be followed by a new beginning resolving the conflict.

FIFTH, the three-year-old Essene Christian Community in Grand Rapids, Michigan, is an example of the types of smaller groups that exist around the nation on the fringe of the Jesus movement. Believing they are divinely called, members follow much of conservative Christian practice, tongue speaking, laying on of hands, etc., but add a belief in the transmigration of souls into various lives. Headed by a young man, Dick Thayer, who believes he has a special revelation from God, the group is planning to move from the city to a forty-family farm near Grand Rapids.

SIXTH, the new mystical religion, the Holy Order of MANS, headquartered in San Francisco, has come to thirty-six cities. Made up mostly of young Jesus People types, male members dress like Catholic priests, while the girls dress in modified nun's robes, minus the headpieces. The leader of the mother diocese in San Francisco, the Rev. Father Andrew Rossi, twenty-nine, from Iron Mountain, Michigan, explained his faith in an interview in his San Francisco office. Rossi, who once attended the Society of the Divine Savior Roman Catholic seminary in St. Nazianz, Wisconsin, for four years, said he came to his current faith after years of searching for peace of mind by a route that led through Eastern religions. "We are Christian," he said, sitting beneath pictures of Jesus and Mary and the sacred heart. With horn-rimmed glasses and an intellectual, friendly manner, he looked very much the part of a typical chancery official. But his is a Christianity not only of the New Testament, he says, but also of the ancient Christian mysteries. Before Jesus there were many mystical orders, among them the Essenes, who lived in the desert and communed with nature and the sun, with elaborate baptism and other rituals. They speak of a Christ consciousness that is distinct from Jesus, the vehicle of the Christ. They accept reincarnation, extrasensory perception, and other practices from the East, but do not emphasize them. Reincarnation is just as acceptable as "the nose on the head," said Rossi, and he recalls his own previous life experience in China and Europe. "All things are in the mind of the Father," he said. "So therefore there is instant communion, if you are willing to open up to him."

MANS is an acronym for mystical terms that members will not reveal. It also stands for mankind. The order conducts a Community Aid Station in San Francisco, a sort of Salvation Army Harbor Light rescue program that feeds 4,000 persons a month and houses twenty men a night. Members are not allowed to drink alcoholic beverages. They can date and marry only with permission. They must give all their possessions to the central house in San Francisco. The founder is Dr. Earl W. Blighton, seventy, a former mechanical engineer who served nondenominational churches in the East before starting the new movement in 1961. Sacraments include "illumination" and "realization of the self." Illumination is "reception of light in the body of the person," said Rossi. And light is defined here, he said, as in science, a vibration of energy that gives direction and vision. The sacrament of realization is "opening of the self to the being or point of God within oneself, a cell in the body of the Father." Besides these two additional sacraments, the order recognizes more traditional sacraments such as baptism, communion, extreme unction, confession, marriage, holy orders (ordination). "Confirmation comes with experience," said Rossi. "When illumination comes, there is plenty of confirmation there."

VI

To go the path of the Jesus People of all types—the regular and the unusual fringe sect types—is to take an unknown road East. Granted, the Jesus People get hung up on Western legalisms at times —verbosity, sacraments and ordinances, right and wrong actions, percentage apportionments (one day worship, contributing a tenth or greater percentage, if not all to the commune, etc.). But the floor-sitting Jesus people, the rejoicing-always crowd, the greater-than-life kids who know there is another world (they're walking in it), the chanters, the singers, the nonrational—caught up in the total mystical embracing of all of life with God, recognizing all within sight, smell and touch as God's creation and the very pure air one breathes as God's incense—these are following an Eastern way.

Jacob Needleman, author of *The New Religions,* feels that through the Eastern religions, as one learns gradually to relate with fuller and fuller reality, through such means as the total consciousness of Zen or disciplines of yoga, one rediscovers the sense of "the gradations of religious life. For while the all-or-nothing principle of faith communicates the ever-present exigency of the search for God, the equally important principles of compassion (in Buddhism) and catholicity (in Christianity) recognize the great forces of resistance that operate upon man in this search." [7] It is their belief in demons and extra forces that leads the Jesus People to accept this gradation concept—there is much to be overcome, in steps. Their recognition of men of charisma—they sort of choose rather than elect their leaders—illustrates that some are more holy than others. The concept of the second baptism of the Holy Spirit and the coming indwelling of the Holy Spirit, bringing certain gifts for some (if not most) further leads them to accept the Eastern mystical ideas of gradations or stages of holiness. "The Eastern cosmic scheme brings back the idea of *levels* of intelligence and consciousness in the universe. And since man in this scheme is an image of the universe, a real basis is provided for us to ask: At what level of consciousness do *I* exist? and: at what level of consciousness *may* I exist? This then leads to the idea of inner evolution as a result of spiritual work." [8]

Needleman suggests also that Eastern religion might be bringing a new moral consciousness. Curiously, the Jesus People almost never seem to talk about the Ten Commandments. An exception was Pastor Allen Hansen, but remember Hansen represents an older generation, and he is an ordained Lutheran at that.

(Lutherans, like Luther, are always fighting the battle of interpreting the commandments in the tension between law and grace.) The Jesus People create their own ethic out of faith. They make a direct leap from faith to practice, without logic and without commandments. Certain life styles and fidelity are implicit in faith.

Needleman says that the influence of Eastern religion also brings "the revitalization of the idea that in a spiritual discipline what we call moral rules are really instruments for the production of certain experiences which make the seeker directly aware of the need for the transcendent inner help in the governance of his life. Thus, the external *Thou Shalt* may be organically displaced by an internal understanding of the reasons for 'sanity' and 'balance' in life." [9]

Says John Groutt, instructor in religion and psychology at Villa-nova (Pennsylvania) University:

Rational theological speculation is irrelevant and dead for these peo-ple. Call it a return to pietism, fundamentalism, or mysticism—it does not matter. It is all of these, but much more. . . . A metanoia (change) occurs wherein lives are dramatically altered, insights permanently gained, experiences traumatic. Meditation without drugs often continues. 'Natural highs' from grooving on nature, music, and people are another common result; a lasting appreciation of the beauty of life and death is another. All of these are reminiscent of the mystical experiences of saints and holy men, and it is difficult if not impossible to distinguish the altered lives of many members of this movement from that of some mystics.[10]

9

Doctrines of the Jesus People

There appear to be two traditions striving to win out in the Jesus People movement—the Baptist and the pentecostal. You can tell which influence prevails as soon as an evangelist warms up and starts jumping and shouting, or as soon as the music gets under way. The pentecostals (the Assemblies of God and other holiness groups) will begin to lift up their arms and wave their hands a little. "Oh, Jesus . . . *aban . . . kanibi . . . olayshun veovkaya un moshevu,* etc." The Baptist-oriented among them, whether they know it or not, keep their hands down. The pentecostals are the ones with the raised hands, for raised hands are a form of special homage to the Holy Spirit descending. The pentecostals derive support for tongue-speaking from Acts 2:3, "tongues as of fire"; Acts 10:46, "they heard them speaking in tongues"; I Corinthians 12:10, "various kinds of tongues"; and a reference to tongue-speaking as one of the special gifts of the spirit, along with teaching, healing, prophesying, etc. in I Corinthians 12:28.

If there is one thing the more matter-of-fact Baptists (and other main-line Protestant traditionalists related to Western European pietism and reform movements) can't stand, it is tongue-speaking. Also there is one thing the conservative and evangelical do insist on —it is "eternal security." Today's youth do not know what that means, although curiously, in a list of doctrines submitted to some

Jesus People groups for rating, at least one marked "eternal security" as important.

Eternal security is the doctrine that "once saved, you are always saved." Baptists use such proof texts as: "And I give them eternal life, and they shall never perish, and no one shall snatch them out of my hand" (Jn. 10:28); "For I know whom I have believed and I am sure that he is able to guard until that Day what has been entrusted to me" (2 Tim. 1:12); and "For I am sure that neither death, nor life, nor angels . . . will be able to separate us from the love of God in Christ Jesus" (Rom. 8:38, 39).

Opponents of the idea of eternal security depend on verses such as: "But he who endures to the end will be saved" (Mt. 24:13); and "For it is impossible to restore again to repentance those who have once been enlightened, who have tasted the heavenly gift, and have become partakers of the Holy Spirit . . . if they then commit apostasy, for they crucify the Son of God" (Heb. 6:4, 6). Pentecostals believe you have to stay with it to be saved, although there is not much doubt once the Holy Spirit gets hold of you. Still, one has to live in that power to get there.

I sense, and I may be wrong, that attempts by Jesus People leaders and others linked with them to push the concept of the gift of the Holy Spirit to speak in tongues onto the new young Christians may be waning. Efforts by pentecostals early in the game, such as Dave Wilkerson, Tony and Sue Alamo, Morris Cerullo, and others, and late arrival but influential Pat Boone, may not represent the total "now" picture. The Campus Crusade types, particularly Southern Baptists such as Arthur Blessitt, Calvary Baptist Church, the J. C. Light and Power Co., and the no-nonsense Southern Baptist Barry Wood, youthful pastor of First Baptist, Beverly Hills, who has opened a Christian night club on Sunset Strip, are now all being counted in the shaping of theological expressions.

Sometimes the Jesus People will speak out openly against excessive use of tongues. Sometimes you just feel, when there is an absence of tongue speaking or a very quiet interjection of it by someone in a corner, that "tongues" is not the thing it is supposed to be as recorded by an action seeking photographer or others. But its presence in the movement cannot be ignored.

Among the most frequent tongue speakers are the Children of

God, who, despite their plea for simplicity, are excessive with their tongues. Unlike some pentecostal moguls in the movement, they give their kids plenty of time, which is needed if you really get the tongues thing going. This generous provision of time is one of the reasons for the success of tongue-speaking in the Catholic pentecostal movement. Those Catholic-initiated services allow great periods of meditation and silence, punctuated only by occasional Scripture.

When the Jesus People youths begin to spin their own prayers and move into the more exotic but serious lingo, they usually need a little time to do it up well. While some of them seem to turn on very fast with the strange speaking, it really comes out of an extended period of build-up. The Children of God, as they meet all night, with their undercurrent of music and youthful exuberance, combine with the sensitivity of touch—the holy kisses, the joining of arms on shoulders in a snake dance, the holding of hands—reach peak emotion. Tongue-speaking becomes a constant of the long emotional high. Tongue-speaking is so much a part of their lives, that Sister Bethia—one of seven who tried to convert me the night I spent with the Children of God in Los Angeles—could babble in tongues almost between bites of ice cream, it was so much a part of her style. Her eyes twinkling, she'd interrupt a sentence for a little tongue-speaking, then later, without batting an eye, join the sentence where she left off. Mrs. Justus, ordained in an independent pentecostal church, former sponsor of the Children of God in Detroit, called the use of tongue-speaking by some of the youths, particularly the new converts, who catch on quickly to the tongue-speaking of their mentors in the Children of God, "a flesh trip and artificial. How can these kids come out of a pop festival and before dawn have the Holy Ghost?" she asked. "I tell you, you have to be clean, and it takes time for God to pour in the Spirit."

Mike Miller, of the J. C. Light and Power Co., in Los Angeles, critical of the Children of God and other similar groups, declared that the J. C. Light and Power Co. people have "no tongue-speaking at all. Something like that, we'd have to have an interpreter. If there is a gift of tongues, we'd want to know, too, if it causes love. The gift of tongues is a more earthly language," and he referred to I Corinthians 14:59, which is a put-down of tongue-speaking: "He who prophesies is greater than he who speaks in tongues," and to I Corinthians 14:6: "If I come to you speaking in tongues, how shall I benefit you, unless I bring you some revelation or knowledge or prophecy or teaching?" The real put-down is verse 4: "He who speaks in a tongue edifies himself." Says Miller: "I Corinthians 14 is a good guideline. It warns against the tongues becoming an end. The greatest gift is love. . . . I personally would pray that the Lord keep them quiet."

Sammy Tippit, of the House of the Risen Son, Chicago, former associate of Baptist Arthur Blessitt, declared, "We are heavy in the giver, not the gifts. We do not push tongues." Jack Sparks of the Christian World Liberation Front says people can be expected to "trip out on certain things. One thing lacking is a broad solid teaching." Duane Pederson, of the Hollywood *Free Paper,* says, "I have no hassle with those who speak in tongues. It's in the Bible. If people choose to use it, it's there. I do not practice it in public. I feel many of those things divide the body of Christ. And if we propagate those idiosyncrasies, it divides instead of bringing people together."

I

It is not by accident that the theme song of the Jesus movement —the one you hear the most—talks about lifted hands. Based on Psalm 63:3-4, and called "Thy Loving Kindness" it appears in a June, 1969, collection (third edition) called the *Psalter,* edited by Arlene Breashers, published by the Bethany Missionary Association, 612 Dawson, Long Beach. An introduction to the book indicates that the songs are Holy Spirit inspired, with the theme of the ninety-page book based on Ephesians 5:19—"Addressing one another in psalms and hymns and spiritual songs, singing and making melody to the Lord with all your heart." The songs are all selected Psalms. Most fit into a pentecostal framework easily. "Thy loving kindness is better than life. Thy loving kindness is better than life. My lips shall praise thee, thus will I bless thee: I will lift up my hands in thy name," and the hands go up in pentecostal symbolism at this point. But Pastor Hansen, the Lutheran minister at Renewal House in Los Angeles, avoids the pentecostal imagery and imparts a significantly different symbolism, by having his youths hold hands; at the appropriate point, they raise their hands *together,* linked, and he leads them on to sing, "We will lift up our hearts . . . lives. . . ."

Calvary Chapel, near Costa Mesa, spawner of eight Jesus communes, and one of the hottest things in the Jesus movement in the Los Angeles area, is supposed to be strong on manifestations of the gifts of the Holy Spirit. But it is a Baptist church, and I found them very self-conscious about the "gifts" and curbing them—rather, their excesses—with a subtle and quiet technique. There was no risk of the sensational, and in good Baptist style, the approach was very individualistic at one of their Friday night sessions overflowing with 400 kids. Eventually only about five hands went up in pentecostal style, then ten more, in the final singing. Ken Gulliksen, youth minister, Nordic, white-blond-haired, concluded the worship service by having the youths link their arms, and all sang "Our Father who art in heaven. . . ." The service ended abruptly—or promptly—and Gulliksen announced for those who were interested that there would be an "afterglow" service. "If you come to receive the power of the Holy Spirit," he said, inviting those interested to come up front, where they sat on the carpeting of the chancel and in the aisles, "Praise the Lord. But don't come for the gifts. We don't come for gifts, but for power. We'll praise God *once* and receive it. Your experience is different. He loves us individually. . . . Jesus is here now . . . he is the one to baptize you." Then he knelt and laid hands individually on each of the some fifty youths who were seated on the floor. His prayers could not be heard in the sanctuary, and in the silence, with no audible expression or sensationalism of tongues, the youths received the Holy Spirit. No jumping up and down. No clicking of the heels. An abomination, no doubt, to some of the Jesus People pentecostal types who accompany the giving of the gifts with much activity.

II

I asked some of the Jesus houses to rate doctrines from a list I suggested. The list was purposely a mixture of doctrines and nondoctrinal ideas, specifics and generalities. The response was revealing in several ways. Out of some thirty houses responding, only about twenty-one felt that doctrine was important or could be rated.

Those who rated the doctrines and ideas gave a pretty good picture as to what is all-important, what is negotiable or adaptable, and what is of no importance at all.

Most important doctrine to the Jesus People is Christ. "Accepting Christ" was by far the most important idea and was marked number one by fourteen of the twenty-one houses. Also four said the "divinity of Christ" was of first importance, thus making eighteen out of twenty-one putting Christ as the first item of importance. Receiving the highest rating as second choice was again "accepting Christ," tied with "love." Five houses selected each as their second choice. Representatives of houses who placed "accepting Christ" in second place had chosen for their first place: "love" (Love Inn, Freeville, New York); "divinity of Christ" (Turning Point, Wailuku, Hawaii; His House, Indianapolis; St. James Community, Portage, Wisconsin); "Bible as inerrant" (House of the Son of David, Denver). Choices for third place were more widespread, with five selecting "Bible as inerrant" and three selecting "love." The rest of the third place choices were spread among ten categories.

Here's what the Jesus houses were asked on question number five of the questionnaire: "Name five most important doctrines or tenets in order of preference of your group (mark most important number 1, second most important 2, etc.)." And these were the items they were to check:

Bible as inerrant	Divinity of Christ	Eternal Security
Accepting Christ	Baptism	Existence of Church
Heaven	Lord's Supper	Creation by God
Hell	Virgin Birth	Love
Spirit Filling	Sanctification	Social Justice
Christ-like living	Gifts of the Spirit	_____ other

The respondents added three items of their own in the rating. These were: "Read Bible," "Bible as the Propositional Revelation of God," and "Repentance."

Also significant in a questionnaire such as this (despite the intentional overlapping, which is designed to make the respondent think and struggle with his choices) are the items that receive no support whatsoever. Receiving absolutely no points whatever were "hell," "virgin birth," and "existence of church." This correlates with the way the Jesus People talk. They talk, as we have seen, of their alienation from present institutions, and in a doctrinal rating, the church's existence correspondingly is of no importance to them. Their eyes are on Jesus and salvation, and there is no thought of hell. This might be a sleeper as to hidden elements in the Jesus movement—perhaps pointing to an unconscious affinity with the mentality of the Eastern religions, which do not have a hell. If the Jesus movement proliferates into sects, they could be of the type such as the Jehovah's Witnesses on the one hand and the Unitarian-Universalist on the other, not to mention the many occult and metaphysical varieties available, which do not recognize a literal hell.

Rating their first five choices on a point system, the Jesus People houses responding established the following (five points assigned for a first place choice, four for a second, three for third place, two for fourth, and one for fifth) order of doctrinal priorities:

Accepting Christ	93	points
Divinity of Christ	37	"
Love	37	"
Bible as Inerrant	29	"
Christ-like Living	27	"
Spirit Filling	25	"
Baptism	17	"
Social Justice	12	"
Sanctification	6	"
Eternal Security	4	"
Witnessing	4	"
Read Bible	4	"
Repent	3	"
Gifts of the Spirit	3	"
Heaven	2	"
Lord's Supper	2	"
Bible as Propositional Revelation of God	1	"
Creation by God	1	"

A lack of concern with setting doctrines in rank order is indicated in some of the comments: for example, Jim Kaminski, secretary of the Jesus House, Champaign, Illinois, did not rate the items in the doctrinal question, and said "All Scripture is profitable for doctrine. There is no order. We should be filled with all the fullness of God" (Eph. 3:19). Marty Irvine, elder of the House of Life, Buffalo, New York, on the other hand, filled out the rating but said "It's hard to give them 'degrees.' They're *all* important." Said Paula Brody, deaconess, Hosanna House, Eugene, Oregon: "All are important in the Christian life," and she, too, declined to rate them. Since, for instance, the references to the Spirit and "eternal security" are not mutually inclusive, according to the old Baptist and pentecostal difference, to say they are all OK perhaps underscores the impreciseness—if not openness—of Jesus People on doctrinal matters. John Kachelmyer, of the Christian Mission to Youth, Inc., of New Mexico (Albuquerque) is aware of the potential differences and incompatibility, at least in a formal doctrinal sense, of items in the list. He says: "We could not possibly give any order of importance. All these are important. We do not, however, believe in eternal security in the Baptist sense."

The Rev. Dr. Henlee H. Barnette, professor of Christian ethics, Southern Baptist Seminary, Louisville, Kentucky, sums up the general theological significance of the Jesus People from the viewpoint of traditional concerns and terminology: The Jesus People movement, he says, "gives Christology a central place in the movement, it stresses eschatology, a note long lost in theology; it stresses the Holy Spirit, another religious reality lost to the more 'respectable' denominations; also it emphasizes love for neighbor and radical *koinonia* (fellowship)."

It is possible to see other theological themes in the Jesus People movement. There are unwritten and unformulated doctrines in the movement, possibly because the Jesus People go strong on Scripture. There are no guidelines of formulated dogma, creeds, or decrees of ecumenical councils. Besides their theology that derives from selected verses, particularly those that enunciate the need of faith in Jesus (e.g. Jn. 3:16, etc.), their style reflects reliance on a variety of verses and not necessarily ones they quote the most often. Their style indicates the importance of Bible injunctions such as "do not look dismal" (Mt. 6:16), and "where two or three are gathered in my name, there am I in the midst of them" (Mt. 18:20) and

"You shall love your neighbor as yourself" (Mt. 22:39) and "be of good cheer, I have overcome the world" (Jn. 16:33).

The unexpressed theology of the Jesus People consists largely of laying hold of these verses which support their inherent tendency to create a climate of *celebration* and joy before the Lord, to live together in *fellowship* in the name of Jesus in communes, to recognize *responsibility* for the needs of others and to maintain always a stance of *hope*. It is possible, too, that as the doctrine of the Jesus People who believe in the imminent return of Jesus evolves, a less cataclysmic view of the future might emerge, linking all the categories of celebration, fellowship, and responsibility with joyous hope. "My impression is that the Jesus People phenomenon represents one more attempt to see and to communicate profound meaning in contemporary life," says Dr. Hobbs Walter, of the State University of New York. "It's another affirmation that life is not hopeless, despite appearances."

Because the Jesus People lack precise formulations and because their style is so dramatic, Dr. Hobbs notes also that there is "the danger common to all evangelistic efforts, namely, that the form will become the substance. Just as middle-class evangelicalism is often just religion and more middle-class than evangelical, so too the Jesus People movement faces the prospect of hippie evangelicalism, more street life than evangelical. Neither middle-class life style nor street-life style is in itself laudable or damnable (though certain elements of each society are), but both are poor seconds to the life of faith per se. Yet they can easily supersede the latter if 'promoted.'"

When style is more obvious than doctrine, then the style can become the doctrine, Dr. Hobbs argues. But it should also be noted that style can also be an important factor in recovering lost precepts. Celebrative and community styles of concern could just accidentally correspond to the original doctrines and teachings of Jesus. Perhaps the Jesus People are showing a new way to basic doctrine apart from an apostolic handing down of tradition. Their experiential life-styles may be as valid, if not more so, than carefully-watched and sometimes carefully-tampered-with historic traditions. An over-preoccupation with style may not be bad doctrine at all, nor detrimental nor indicative of an eclipse of faith.

In a sense, there is a little bit of the insight of the latter day ecumenists who in striving to get the Consultation on Church Union off the ground recognized that unity will not now come by super-structure and compromising of traditions and forms but from a lived experience. Consider COCU's draft plan on unity as it relates to the parishes of the nine denominations considering merger:

In all of this shared life of worship, we foresee for the early stages of the united church a period of mutual exploration and discovery of one another's traditions. In this period, use may be made of any of the forms of public worship now generally in use in the constituting churches (although no congregation may be required to use any such form). It is our hope and aim that in due course new disciplines may emerge, representative of the discoveries we have all made in separation from one another and others we can only make when we are one.[1]

III

The Jesus People bring to ecumenism and the doctrines of church unity the lived experience of faith, and with their own heterogeneous background (Jewish, Protestant, Roman Catholic, etc.), their cultural as well as spiritual input into unifying Christendom may be far greater and more effective than the belabored efforts of bureaucrats in the nine limited traditions of COCU or in smaller merger groups. "The stress of selflessness, morality and brotherly concern is a helpful approach to bring mankind together when so many forces seem to be tearing people apart," says Dr. John Paul Eddy, of Loyola University of Chicago. "Another feature of this [Jesus People] movement is to challenge others who are lacking spiritual experiences to new frontiers of faith."

Miss April Daien, who is dubbed "the resident freak" on the *Arizona Republic* (Phoenix) newspaper, because of her work with the counterculture, including the Jesus People, notes that their preoccupation with total commitment is akin to total annihilation. "Drugs for some of them is a way to seek annihilation," she said. "And total commitment is a push to annihilation." I suppose you could read "annihilation" several ways. They are so frustrated, so disillusioned, that drugs or Jesus in absolute forms are a way of suicide. Or you could read "annihilation" in a more mystical sense, as an attempt to seek absorption into something. Again, if you read it this way, here is another instance of the affinity of the Jesus movement for the thought of the East. With Jesus, annihilation, an absorption, is an immediate attainment; with nirvana and other states of the Eastern life, absorption into overall consciousness and nothingness takes a long route. Yet the Indian mystics, like the Gnostic mystics and the desert mystics of Christianity, do seek to tap the mind of God through ascent in spiritual meditation and discipline. They share with society, perhaps again working from common frustrations, a common goal and a common route, if not in the discipline, at least in the process of annihilation of self and total commitment to the One, the Overall, God, or his Incarnation, his Mystical Body.

Prophecy is strong as a biblical concept, but, here again, the Jesus People have a haziness, plus a degree of tolerance, concerning the nature of the last days. Some believe a great tribulation will come before the return of Christ; others believe that Christ will snatch them out at the end of it, or perhaps midway. Reference is heard on occasion to "the latter rain," meaning the pouring out of the spirit on all flesh and in which "your sons and daughters shall prophesy, your old men shall dream dreams, your young men shall see visions" (Joel 2:28; see also Acts 2:16–17—references which some Jesus People feel apply to the Jesus movement). Yet few of the Jesus communes are ever named after Joel and its concepts, a good indication that prophecy is not paramount in the movement.

The lack of defined doctrine and the emphasis on the experiential lead one to note a variety of strands in this strange young ecumenism that on the surface looks so much like a pentecostal revival but in analysis looks like a much broader movement that cannot be contained, no matter who is holding the bag or bags (pentecostal, Baptist, etc.) to catch it. Jews and Catholics in the movement probably bring a distinctive influence, as others do. Many houses report a variety of religious backgrounds. The New Slant in Chappaqua, New York, for example, numbers fifty persons, with 10 per cent of Jewish background and 30 per cent Roman Catholic, despite sponsorship by a Presbyterian church. The sense of totality of Jesus People is akin to Hebrew thought, which linked body and soul and the mind and the emotions. It may well prove to be a highly significant influence as the Jesus People seek to link Greek and Oriental dualism, with their sense of the struggle between God and the Devil, and the transience of this life, with a concern for reform in this life. Their means at present are experiential rather than political or activist, but this does not preclude developments in a more political or concrete direction (see last chapter). In the Jesus People movement, there are Roman Catholic concepts of natural law. The Jesus People tend to oppose abortion. A child—fetus, or what have you—lives by the will of God. Said recently-married Brian, of Emmaus House, Toronto, "Children are a blessing from God. He gives them to you or doesn't give them to you for some reason. You could take all the pills you wanted and if God wanted you to have a child, you'd have one." [2]

In comparison with Jewish and Roman Catholic youth organizations in the counter-culture religious scene, the Jesus People have their own sense of polity. The Jewish "havurah," or fellowship movement, seeks a deeper faith beyond buildings and fundraising campaigns, but it has not centered on a "person," nor has it entered a communal stage as the Jesus People have.

The Catholic charismatic, or Catholic pentecostal, movement is, as we have noted, duller and more formal than the Jesus People movement. Centered in Ann Arbor, Michigan, having been brought there by former students at Duquesne University, Pittsburgh, and Notre Dame, South Bend, Indiana, the Word of God Catholic charismatic community is not transient, as are the Jesus People, but is located in fixed parishes. It has developed its own ecclesiology and structure, far beyond the simplicity and spontaneity of the Jesus People. Emphasis is strong on "renewal" of the faith instead of "rebirth." Participation in one's own church on Sunday is encouraged, as opposed to the Jesus People's general ignoring of the established church. The Word of God community has two ruling "co-ordinators" (original members Ralph Martin and Steve Clark) and nine other co-ordinators who help direct four area subcommittees which have closed meetings on Mondays in comparison to the large public meeting on Thursdays. Under them are ten "servants" and eight "handmaidens" who may be compared to deacons and deaconesses in the Bible. These help in administration and in publishing a monthly magazine named *New Covenant*. The Word of God has thirty houses of communes or partial communes. The whole structure is referred to as a "system of headship." There is a creed and courses (referred to as "preparation" and "foundation" courses) that compare to catechetical training before membership is accomplished in a creed-reciting rite.

Listen to and watch Jesus People communion services for hints of their doctrinal beliefs. In that House of Emmaus, much as in houses on the West Coast and in the smaller communes, members settle on the floor in a small room at 8:15 A.M. Sunday.

They pray the Lord's Prayer.

A black youth, Frank Clear, twenty, prays for "all of the body to love one another."

They sing a song with guitar, thanking God for "setting us free like eagles flying about the clouds . . . may the body stand together with no division . . . we are nothing—just lumps of clay . . . may we walk in the Spirit . . . chastise us . . . we want to be ready when you call out . . . Hallelujah . . . we give you the praise and the glory."

Then a youth, Clarence Crossman, eighteen, rises and reads by the faint sunlight:

"Take, eat, this is my body, which is broken for you: this do in remembrance of me." And "This is the new testament in my blood: this do ye, as oft as ye drink it, in remembrance of me. For as often as ye eat this bread, and drink this cup, ye do shew the Lord's death till he come" (I Cor. 11:24-26).

Acting leader Terry Baker prostrates himself on the floor, his face in a pillow.

"Make yourself real to us," one prays.

"Deepen our love for you and for one another."

Terry takes the cup of wine (a plain large wine glass) and the plain white bread and distributes it: "May we take these blessings with us into the world and rejoice in our hearts and glorify your name."

A youth next to me speaks very softly in tongues, as if not to offend the others.

Clear prays again: "I pray for deeper love . . . that all of us brethren might grow in love with you."

The guitarist, a former night club singer and comedian in Montreal, who looks a lot like pictures of the round-faced, martyred German theologian Dietrich Bonhoeffer with eyeglasses, sings in the background, and all join in: "Hallelujah," and softly chanting, "Jesus is Lord."

Posters on the wall declare: "Awake O sleeper, arise from among the dead, and Christ will shine on you and give you light."

Clear starts a song: "Oh how I love Jesus, because he first loved us."

The guitarist prays: "Give us patience to be good listeners and speakers for Christ . . . and to realize all is possible if we trust him."

Terry: "Teach us, Father, to rest in thy grace today and not (live) from a vine that is green."

Clear: "Teach us, Lord, to be meek."

Then—

Terry: "Is it possible to have a laying on of hands from a distance, since time and space are nothing for God?"

And they pray for a sister in another part of the country.

Here are elements of traditional Protestantism (spontaneous prayers), Catholicism (wine, prostration in prayer), pentecostalism (some tongues), Eastern mysticism (transcending space and time), and Judaism (ethical concern for right living).

There is a curious scarcity of faith healing among Jesus youths, although they do pray for one another's healing, and there is some testimony along this line. But in my travels I recall very few direct attempts at faith healing in their sessions. Possibly these healthy, ruddy-cheeked youngsters (although some of the newcomers are pale from a past of drugs) are not thinking too much about illness. They are losing grandmothers and the like, but death and illness have not been too close to them. Splitting off the faith healing, while they are debating the efficacy of tongue-speaking, makes it more difficult to say these young people are all headed for the Assemblies of God and related pentecostal camps. The Jesus People fit no bag yet, although some groups, notably Assemblies of God evangelists, are holding out the bag to catch them. But the pentecostals may be just snipe hunting. The Jesus People may prove to be a different kind of animal, and the prescribed bags of immediate past generations—those of the pentecostals as well as the Baptists and others—may prove inadequate for a faith that is (1) consciously trying to get back to Christian primitivism and (2) unconsciously joining a larger counterculture, Eastern and Western orientated, in demanding new institutions.

10

Where the Money Comes From

The implications of strings on contributed money must be considered, and the over-all economics, no less, without which—spirit or no spirit—the Jesus People cannot continue. How strong are the Jesus People economically? What influence does the means of financing have on the direction they are going?

There are dozens of ways in which the Jesus houses—the communes and coffee houses—and special Jesus ministries, such as festivals, church raps, street evangelization, and the "road shows" of Arthur Blessitt's and others are financed. While sometimes it seems that one man might have a corner on the Jesus movement, so that it would rise with him and fall without him, there is such great diversity that the demise of any one person would make little difference. The variety of means of financing indicates a certain creativity and independence and the lack of any central control of the movement at this moment. The main question is what kind of money is coming into the movement and whether that money is influencing the development of the movement. At this stage, again, the answers are various, as different kinds of money are coming in. Whether somebody with enough funds and interest in the movement can cleverly set up independent liaisons with separate Jesus houses and buy up the movement under the pretense that God is providing remains to be seen. Jesus People are often asked if they are a front for the CIA, elders have told me. They deny this. They don't deny in many instances, however, that businessmen who are professed Christians in various areas are putting up the money. Naively, perhaps, they believe that any money coming their way comes from God, even if God's proxy has Mafia, Birch or extremist connections of one sort or another.

I

Why do big men in the nation's corporations put money into Jesus People operations? Here are the straights—the 11 A.M., pew-sitting, dressed-up worshipers; the Sunday-school book types; the family men with shoes and two garages, who sit in straight chairs at Wednesday prayer meetings. They are the antithesis of the Jesus People movement. They and their secular suburban counterparts are among the reasons the Jesus People exist. As the Rev. Dr. Ronald E. Osborn, of Christian Theological Seminary, Indianapolis, explains, "Man does not live by bread alone, nor by the sophisticated affluence of suburbia, nor by the exaggerated self-indulgence of 'California living.' His spiritual hunger cannot be fed by materialism or by churches which major in sedate propriety. In this movement, young people may find raw gospel, but apparently it is gospel." The Jesus People, however, are willing to pass over the contradictions of accepting their money by saying these businessmen are (1) participants in the faith, although espousing a different style, and God is using them, or (2) God is just using them, whoever they are, as God has used good and bad men throughout history.

Why the straight businessman, whose very church and style is threatened by the freak holy young people, should take an interest in them may be explained also by fear. Anything to corral these types perhaps appeals to him, even though, being a parent, he may also genuinely want to help. Yet the Christian businessman also thinks in a single track on such things. It surely must make him happy to hear glowing testimonies from these young people, who incidentally tend to get cleaned up and shaven and thus look more like the straighter businessmen, in compromise if not in a total restyling (you still can't get shoes on many Jesus People's feet).

The businessman also wants power and uniformity even in his church life. Most probably do not expect to make money on it (although it may be another story for the radio and evangelist hucksters, whose motives may be more complex and difficult to probe). If there is material gain for the businessman, it comes from propagating a style of life, his *status quo*. Or when southern California businessmen get into the long mixture of religion and politics, as some are doing, there come some questions, which, incidentally, Dan McCurry, of the Dietrich Bonhoeffer House, Chicago, and former member of the United Church of Christ Board of Homeland Ministries staff, will be exploring in a just-started year-long project.

Good Christian businessmen I know and have known—including some good friends—have the larger interest of society in mind. Yet to them, as I suppose to most people, the ideal society conforms to their ideal. Christ only. A nation under God. Clean. Quiet. Moral. Preferably white, but not necessarily so, if all are in their place. And so on. This is to say, Christian business money in the Jesus People movement may have political implications, although surprisingly I find the Jesus People a-political at the moment. There is some talk of Communism being of the Devil, helped along by the intriguing study of prophecy by Hal Lindsey (*The Late Great Planet Earth*), and there is some revival of feeling against the National Council and World Council of Churches. But the Jesus People seem to care little about these old hang-ups. And they could hardly care less about conservative boycotts of the National Council of Churches related to the Revised Standard Version of the Bible. They themselves pick up any version of the Bible, as we have seen, and the observer finds the French-Catholic-prepared Jerusalem Bible one of the most common study Bibles on their shelves. The old politics of the Christian conservative are not really the Jesus People's concern. Yet some businessmen may believe that money and indirect control and leading could bring them around. Historically, church power and uniformity have been the goals of Christian businessmen in Christian education, according to Elliott Wright's and Robert Lynn's *The Big Little School,* as we have seen.

An increasingly important reason for the sudden interest of Christian businessmen in the Jesus People movement probably is the over-all change and precariousness of overseas missions. With most mission fields now operated by local national Christians and with the continued instability of the Third World, in which governments look more favorably upon missionaries who have talents other than mere gospel preaching, the Christian businessman can rightly wonder if his money going overseas can make good, decent Christians out of the world's "Hottentots." Now with the counter-culture natives in all of their primitiveness existing right in the back yard of the businessman in suburbia, the missionary challenge is to bring some of the evangelistic and/or patronizing spirit back home. Why not win some of the crude white and black natives? "My God, my son and daughter, or at least some of the kids they have to mix with, heaven forbid—to Jesus?" It works. They can be converted. Pragmatism. "And listen to these kids' glorious testimonies. God is at work. Amen."

Thus it is no surprise, for instance, to learn that The Master's House in Lansing, Michigan, is under the wing of Calvary Christian Crusades. According to a member of the house, Calvary Christian Crusades is sponsored by Richard Welch, a Lansing steel broker, and Crusades supports two African missionaries as well as The Master's House. House of Peace, Albuquerque, New Mexico, according to John M. Kachelmyer, director of the sponsoring agency, Christian Mission to Youth, Inc., and an eight-year missionary to youth in Japan, is supported "by contributions from interested private persons and churches, mostly from a base of support gained through the mission in Japan." All in the same bag?

Land developer and oilman F. H. Larsen, a member of the Calvary Church, Palisades, is one of the men behind the J. C. Light and Power Co. Larsen, according to house manager Mike Miller, became a Christian in revivals conducted by Lindsey, a former river-boat captain and Campus Crusade leader for ten years. The budget to date for the program and house, purchased three years ago, has been $300,000. The nineteen fellows (only three of them bearded) and seventeen girls live in the big Spanish-style mansion with sunken yard and gardens on a hill of mansions and small, pasteled apartment complexes. Each youth pays $125 a month to live in the house "which is better than living in a dorm, which is $138." About twenty-five are students. On Wednesday nights some 400 youths gather for a Bible study, usually on the grass of the University of California, Los Angeles, or crowded into the great rooms and halls of the former fraternity house.

Christian businessmen joining with Youth for Christ and the Grace Bible Institute pay the bills at Omaha's two Jesus People centers, the Christian Brotherhood and the Soul Concern Coffee House. Mostly Youth for Christ had a hand in launching the Lighter Side of Darkness House, Springfield, Illinois, according to the director, Tom Richardson, with other contributions "by interested individuals." Landlords help out at the Christian Community Center of the Cleveland Jesus Center. "Two people gave us $3,000 total, and the seller dropped his price $10,000, then gave us $10,000 to complete the down payment," says the director, Joel Kischel, who has a Lutheran background. A retired businessman, with the aid of some of his colleagues, supports the Twenty-third Psalm House in Nashville.

At Sheepfold House, Milwaukee, the annual budget is estimated at $36,000 a year (there is a coffee house program in a separate building besides the commune), but members decline to say where the money comes from, except that God provides. But on any evening you can find a car dealer in straight tie and brown coat talking to the small group at a Sheepfold coffee house or a businessman conducting a Bible study. The Milwaukee people also make money by sponsored "hunger hikes," with the money being used to run a bus and buy a farm. Jim Palosaari, head of the Milwaukee movement, acknowledges the support of the Full Gospel Businessmen's Fellowship for his rallies, and has passed an offering plate at the fellowship's meetings, according to a report in the Milwaukee *Journal.* In Washington, ten businessmen met and prayed for help in deciding what to do. They opened the Agape Coffee House and two communes, one of the communes being upstairs over an art and curio shop run by one of the ten. The wife of a second-hand store owner and herself an evangelist paid the way and set up the commune for the Children of God in Detroit, as we have seen. Carlos Alonso launched his El Shaddai House, in Bellaire, Texas, with the money he obtained by selling his business and "also from brothers and sisters." Donations and the soda machine only keep the coffee house program of the Turning Point in Wailuku, Hawaii, going. Local store owners donate the furniture, coffee and other items for the Underground Fish in Grand Rapids, Michigan, with the rent for the store-front put up by two Army veterans. Another former serviceman, Jim Robinson, who was a Navy chaplain, has the backing of city officials and a team of psychologists, doctors and school officials, as well as the use of a restaurant for the His Way movement in Concord, California. Carl Furioso's social action Jesus People project of feeding the poor in Seattle acknowledges a $15,000 gift—in two takes—by an area lady.

II

Many churches are putting money into the Jesus movement, and if they are typical churches, money from businessmen would flow through this channel. The United Methodist Church in Greensburg, Kentucky, hired a youth to work with recent young converts from a revival for the summer, according to a *Christianity Today* report on small-town activity. In Arnold, Nebraska, following another revival, thirteen Bible study groups were set up by laymen. And "meetings at a Baptist church in Nortonville, Kentucky, ran six weeks after the young people took over." [1]

First Presbyterian, Flint, Michigan, bought a storefront, once a tobacco and pipe shop, and used it for worship by youths, most of them straight, but some freaks. The New Slant in Chappaqua, New York, is sponsored by the local Presbyterian Church and staffed with volunteers. Atlanta's First Baptist Church and three Southern Baptist agencies in Atlanta hired Don Rhymes, former missionary in New York City, to head up The Aurora (New Dawn) in Atlanta's freak district. The Tulsa (Oklahoma) Christian Fellowship, when it was organized as a congregation in 1970, voted to pass up acquiring a building in favor of going where the action would be, according to the Tulsa *Daily World*. Members of that church would go up and down the street and ask questions for a survey, among other approaches, in order to talk with youths. Their pastor is the Rev. Bill Sanders who went to the TCF after being booted out by a Tulsa Baptist church for speaking in tongues. First Baptist Church, Beverly, Massachusetts, sponsors the White Whale for Bible study and prayer sessions in a house adjoining the church. The West End Baptist Church, Galveston, Texas, sponsors a Jesus barn, the Red House, where "soul" sessions are held by Rusty Draper, director of programming and disc jockey for radio station KILE. The Methodist Church of Mill Valley, California, provides overnight sleeping quarters with rap sessions for fifteen street youths sponsored by an interfaith ministry, the Street Ministry of Southern Marin County, involving eight churches. Wollaston (Massachusetts) Congregational, Baptist and Methodist churches are setting up a beach ministry. Fifteen Southern Baptist churches got behind evangelist Lee Humphrey to open up a ministry to the hippies in a former New Orleans bank building.

A variety of church coffee houses attract the Jesus People, and even some old-style missions, such as the Yonge Street Mission in Toronto, which once served only alcoholics, now have massive coffee house programs in new ultra modern surroundings on week nights, as regular evangelists hassle youths for the faith. First Baptist, Houston, spent $53,000, with $9,000 of it on buses, raised "from men of the church" and from offerings at the SPIRENO (Spiritual Revolution Now) rallies of Richard Hogue, twenty-four. "The Jesus movement is a great opportunity for churches, which can accept kids as they are and present them Christ, to ground these youngsters in the Word of God and provide a stabilized spiritual force that will have an impact for generations to come," Hogue said. "The Jesus movement has invaded the churches as well as other aspects of life. I think we have ample evidence of that."

Money for some of the biggest and showiest efforts of the Jesus movement come from the kinds of persons who have always made funds available in this century for sudden new movements. In a 1970 article by William C. Martin, assistant professor of sociology at Rice University, Houston, in the *Atlantic Monthly,* they are called "The God Hucksters of Radio." Martin cites persons of the past and present such as the Rev. Frederick B. Eikerenkoetter (Rev. Ike), C. W. Burpo, Kathryn Kuhlman, the late A. A. Allen, Ten Armstrong, J. Charles Jessup, David Terrell and others.

III

The Jesus People also had a boost from radio personalities and other showmen such as the Rev. Fred Jordan of the Church in the Home, also called the American Soul Clinic, Inc., which originally intended to raise funds for overseas mission groups and then sponsored the Children of God in California and Texas, as we have seen. The Rev. George Bogle, ordained in an independent pentecostal church, who broadcasts Monday through Saturday on FM from 10 to 12 P.M. and seven days a week on FM from 12:15 to 2 A.M., now has a new Jesus People radio program, also on FM, at 9 P.M. Monday through Friday—all in the greater Detroit area. Bogle has two mammoth coffee houses going, either one of which would probably pass as the largest in the nation—one of them a former department store in Pontiac, the other a large building in Detroit. He also has a new restaurant grill in Allen Park, Michigan. At this writing he has just called to ask me in great urgency to help him locate a big apartment building for another commune to take the overflow from his House of Prayer in Detroit, with the new one to be largely for married couples. He has also taken over a former gospel tabernacle building and moved from Mt. Clemens, where he once had a church, to Detroit's more expensive new downtown Lafayette apartment area.

Morris Cerullo's World Evangelism headquarters in San Diego sponsors a series of Youth Action Centers in Southern California, notably at San Diego and Anaheim. These specialize in providing twenty-four-hour telephone counseling to youths, drug seminars and speakers for community programs. Cerullo, who grew up in an Orthodox Jewish orphanage, specializes in Spiritual Breakthrough Crusades around the world. He has attracted to himself people who have been influential, directly or indirectly, in the Jesus People movement—e.g., Harold Bredesen, who has been pastor of the First Reformed Church of Mount Vernon, New York. Bredesen led Pat Boone into the experience of speaking in tongues one evening at sunset above a canyon over the San Fernando Valley, in California, and Boone went on to baptize Jesus People and encourage the movement. Doing public relations for Cerullo and Bredesen and others is Dave Balsiger, a young former California newsman, who helped develop the $14.95 Jesus People watch while on the staff of Melodyland Center in Anaheim. Cerullo appears to be working both sides of the fence, but concentrates on the general rally held in hotels or out in open fields.

Evangelist LeRoy Jenkins brought in two young professional women to coordinate a Spirit of Youth Festival in June, 1971, geared toward Jesus People, at Jenkins' eighty-six-acre ranch in Delaware, Ohio. His helpers were Bernie Orlando, director of the Madison Square Garden International Camper and Trailer Show, and Taffy Douglas, a former model and singer who works as director of women's features for WHIO-TV, Dayton. Miss Orlando said in advance releases that "this festival will be the first great beacon to bring together elements of the Jesus Movement now sweeping the young people of the nation. There is only one man, LeRoy Jenkins, who could bring these young people wandering down the highways of the nation to turn onto Jesus, to turn off drugs." I haven't heard about Jenkins since, nor have I heard his name mentioned among Jesus People. Probably the Jesus People figure Jesus rather than Jenkins could do more for them, but doubtlessly Jenkins and others will keep at it to do what they can with the movement, on the airways and in the tents.

Tony and Sue Alamo, now in Saugus, California, are examples of evangelists who have settled almost entirely for the Jesus People. The unsmiling, unhappy spic 'n' span Tony and Sue have put together a tightly organized and unhappy, but sometimes friendly (they do feed you and give you rides) following of several hundred. Beginning in Hollywood, they were constantly hassled by Hollywood's equally unhappy and persistent police. I was picked up by the Alamos' Christian Foundation bus on a Sunday afternoon at Hollywood Boulevard and Highland and rushed out to the lodge on a mountain side now owned by the Alamos' foundation. The whole thing was unbelievable and eerie. First of all, the kind of crew they picked up. Me, in my Salvation Army tattered get-up;

two freaks; two old ladies, one of them quite a way over the line mentally; one squeamish thirtyish dark-haired girl dedicated to converting the mixed-up older lady; a silent Mexican, the lone middle-aged man; a quiet Spanish girl in dark glasses, etc. I took down the interesting cross play of conversation on the ride out, which lasted about an hour.

More relevant was the conversation that followed after communion in the lodge. The Saugus crowd, with big, club-like Bibles, began to climb, yes literally climb, through the audience for a soul. Fortunately, they left me alone. Perhaps I looked too hardened or too indigent. But the neatly-dressed, quiet Latin fellow next to me was a prime target. He told the mean-looking youth with Bible, "I not feel like it" (coming forward to be saved), and rapidly he was told, "You're one heartbeat from death . . . you never know. Your spirit betrays you . . . come down and pray with us! You've nothing to lose but your sins!" To the man's plea, "Next time," the youth replied, "There's no guarantee of a next time—now! You're not opposed to praying, are you?"

All the while, Sue Alamo looked as if she had just walked out from behind the counter of a main-street candy counter, neat, properly blonde, but mean and expressionlessly down on all the world, particularly kids who don't have money for candy. Her husband, short, stocky, square-shouldered, Sicilian-type Tony, stayed largely in the background in his dapper coat and white polka-dot tie.

People have asked me if I were ever afraid of moving about in disguise among some of the Jesus People heavy types, and often they referred to the Children of God. I had no fear of the Children of God, and I even liked the ones I met despite their strange trips. But I might have been afraid, had I been left alone in the inner sanctum of the Saugus crowd, down by the baptismal lake or in the distant mountaintop commune at night, and been discovered as a reporter in disguise. I had wanted to crash it but had to get back (to white tie and suit) for a prior appointment at Pat Boone's home. I like Phil Tracy's description of the Alamos before they moved out of Hollywood into the hills. Tracy said in an early article on "The Jesus Freaks" in *Commonweal*:

Four or five young musicians are up on the make-do stage and they begin the service with an electronic rendition of "Rock of Ages." Just as they're getting into the hymn, Tony and Susan enter the house. Utter pandemonium ensues. People waving their arms in the air and moaning the way the natives used to moan whenever the volcano blew up in those MGM spectaculars. The last time I saw such adulation was when the Beatles played Shea Stadium to a packed house. A young girl next to me nearly fainted from exhilaration at the sight of the pair. And what a sight they make. Tony looks like a used-car salesman and Susan looks like a used-car salesman's wife. Tony is wearing a bright blue shiny suit that you could comb your hair off. In his late thirties, the paunch is just beginning to show while flecks of grey dot his drill-sergeant's-length hair. Susan is what some people call a "bubble head"; bleached blonde with the curls piled up on top of each other in some kind of synthetic beehive effect. They look like the kind of couple that the Playboy Club turns away for being passe. . . .[2]

Another high-powered person, rather obviously getting more from the Jesus People than he is giving to them, appears to be Arthur Blessitt, whom we have talked about earlier. An overrated Jesus People pioneer, nevertheless he gets a good press. An effective showman—recall his trek across the United States with a cross, his street work in Times Square in New York, and his standing between the opposing Protestant and Catholic groups in Northern Ireland—Blessitt may climb to even greater heights on the evangelistic circuit. Despite the fact that he now has a small building with nothing happening at night at the edge of Sunset Strip, which is as quiet as a cow pasture these days, Blessitt still makes a fund-raising pitch about doing something on the strip. On stationery that has "Arthur Blessitt" in big capital letters and a blurb in smaller but large letters, "minister of Sunset Strip," Blessitt describes under a July 1971 dateline his "fantastic" New York "blitz" on sin for Jesus. "Our God, who parted the Red Sea, who led the Children of Israel across Jordan, and who walked upon the water, has performed a twentieth-century miracle in Times Square." Again, Arthur sees himself not only with Moses but with the walking-on-water Lord himself, at least in associating his acts with theirs and giving equal importance to events of which he is the vehicle and motivator.

Blessitt goes on to beg for funds by referring to great things in Hollywood and implying that he and God are responsible for everything that has happened there. He writes in the fund-raising letter, "Jesus has really moved into Hollywood. There are Bible study groups all over each night. Duane Pederson has done a terrific job in holding free Jesus Festivals. . . . Of course, the great miracle is the first Jesus Nightclub called Right On, where there is good food, good entertainment from the best gospel singers, and good preaching. Many have been saved since its opening on June 25th. Ed Human, who was the director of His Place, is now the Director of Right On." Blessitt goes on to ask for money: "It is through your support that outreaches at Sunset Strip and Times Square are provided. We trust that God will lead you to respond in a financial manner to the needs before us." The money is to be sent to Arthur Blessitt Evangelistic Association, a nonprofit Christian Organization, Hollywood. The miracle in all this, it would seem to me, would be if Duane Pederson or Right On, which is not run by Blessitt despite the defection of Ed Human, ever got any of this money. And it's hard to imagine why Blessitt needs any real money, since his work on Sunset Strip these days consists of a lone Texas school girl in the silent drop-in center, His Place, where the counseling rooms are locked up, talking to one or two people who come in. Sunset Strip is not only a deserted former tourist attraction, but Blessitt's own shell of a building fits the ghostly atmosphere. But there is magic, and apparently money, in conjuring up the name of Sunset Strip and the work that others more or less are still doing there. Money for Blessitt.

The Action Life ministry, a smaller effort, now in Woodland Hills, California, makes its pitch to the conservative-minded churchmen. Who else would know who Hudson Taylor is (missionary to China)? Begins a letter of Action Life: "Dear Friends, It was Hudson Taylor who said. . . ." Enclosed in the mailing of the group, headed by Dave Malkin, a clean-cut young crusader against drugs, are clippings from the Denver *Post,* which point out that a visit of the group in Denver was underwritten by Denver businessmen and a Denver organization, Inter-Church Renewal Ministry.

Duane Pederson has his mailings on coarse blue paper under

the heading of the Hollywood *Free Paper* and the Jesus People raised-finger sign. He talks about growing pains with his paper, whose circulation is over 300,000 according to this letter, and some debts. You can rest assured he does not mention Arthur Blessitt. "Please return the enclosed envelope to me," he says. And, "Thank you for your prayers . . . thank you for your gifts . . . and thank you for your help in clearing up the debts we incurred because 'the love of Christ constraineth us'—and the time is so short! All power thru Jesus."

A number of the Jesus People houses have gone to direct mailings, among them the Koinonia Community started in 1969 in Santa Cruz, California. Their three brochures tell of the community house and its coffee house and boutique and the Koinonia singers, drawn from the twenty-five members, most of them under age twenty-five. The Koinonia brochures also promise free posters and pictures of the singers and suggest that the brochures be regarded as press releases to be used at will. Some houses mail out tracts or Bible literature with their address stamped on. Love-Inn, Freeville, New York, which the New York *Times* says "is one commune with no public relations problem" (its members also speak to Kiwanis Clubs and other groups) has a highly professional brochure that also promotes the elder or director, Scott Ross, and his radio show. Peg Hardesty, secretary-treasurer of the group, a fifty-six-year-old widow, provided a barn and farm for the group, which does not solicit directly. She was a convert from Ross's radio program. They distribute an artistic offset fold-out with Scripture and the credits of Ross in radio work, with his picture. Also included is the New York *Times* article of June 15, 1971, happily entitled " 'Jesus People' Happy With Life in Love Inn."

About the Jesus People who are tied up with public personalities—even though most of the personalities are sincere, if perhaps overzealous and energetic in a capitalist nation that recognizes free enterprise in all walks of life, even religion—James Nolan, of Sonoma County, California, writing for *Ramparts,* warns:

The real issue at stake here is that drug-blown, pop-freaked, ego-defenseless kids, who in their innocence, openness and idealism are truly beautiful, can easily become the victims of a desperate evangelism of any kind—that, just as a handful of Hell's Angels can stomp in and take over a pop festival, a small collection of bell-bottomed Baptists and, at worst, Elmer Gantry's, can begin to redirect whole generations into their scripture-lined tents.[3]

IV

Yet, as we have said concerning abortive attempts of adults to get it all together for the young people, the young people have minds of their own—perhaps emphatically clear after having been blown once by drugs. Increasingly, especially among the independent communes, which comprise most of the movement (receiving money from but not directed by professionals), the Jesus People are devising new and creative ways of self-support. The Jesus People Army in Seattle had a bakery; Smyrna House in Toronto is opening up a TV repair shop; the House of Judah in Atlanta has had a restaurant; the House of Life, Buffalo, New York, runs a Christian construction company (House Life Improvement); His House, Indianapolis, Indiana, has an arts and crafts shop; the Twenty-Third Psalm House, Nashville, Tennessee, after help from local Christian businessmen, is going into the upholstery business; in Spokane, Wash., Carl Parks' newspaper *Truth* asks donations for its issues, rather than being given away as other papers are; Koinonia of Santa Cruz, Calif., has a restaurant, bookstore and gift shop.

The earlier mood of some of the Jesus People made them take literally the Garden of Eden story, which declares that work is a curse (Gen. 3:19; 4:11, 12). Some proponents of this theory, in part, at least, are still around outside the Children of God and Christian Foundation, Saugus, movements. For example, Philip Humphrey, thirty-three. Once a singer with the popular Fendermen, belting out "Mule Skinner Blues," etc., Philip, reared as an Episcopalian, later worked with an aerospace firm in Redondo Beach, California, at $12,000 a year, until he had a falling out with management. Philip was converted by an evangelist who came to his door. What followed was joy and a series of far-out trials, Philip said. Interviewed at the House of Smyrna, Toronto, with his

young wife and children, he told of special knocks on the door
that came when even the eyes of his children reflected how hungry
the family was, and "God provided" food and money through
special friends and visitors. Philip worked a while at the ranch
of two elderly ladies from Palmdale, California, whom he had
met at a prayer meeting. But after three months, Philip felt a special
calling back to Toronto, where his wife once worked as a dancer in
Concord Tavern, one of the places where he had sung in his musical days. In the Toronto interview, as he was gathering his family
into a van at sunset, Philip continued, "I say God is the provider.
When he provides, I go to work." He was asked if work was
indeed a curse. "God cursed the ground and said by the sweat of
the brow man would live. Nothing is wrong with that. God is balanced. He doesn't want you to sit on your can. I like work, but if
he wants me to do other things. . . ." Yet work is not a stranger
at Smyrna House. As you settle down there at an evening or
morning meal, you sit next to young men back from the factory
or mills or construction work. It's so at most houses. The strict
discipline of the houses that requires a constant round of Bible
study, yard work, errands and kitchen work, if you stay around
all day, is enough to make many of the more hardy and husky
males glad to get out of the house and work in a man's world.

It's a desire for work that is pushing a lot of the communes
toward a rural setting. Youths who can turn up a farm through
an inheritance or a few side acres from a relative are very popular
indeed with their peers. Elder Robert Trusty, twenty-four, who
came into the Jesus People movement through Lonnie Frisbee,
twenty-two, youth pastor at Calvary Chapel, Costa Mesa, California, said at Christian House, Vacaville, California, which he
supervises, that he is splitting off for Lebanon, Tennessee. A relative is providing a farm. "My mother's house in the country was
vacant," says Meg Dupee, of the St. James Community, Route 3,
Portage, Wisconsin, "so we began to pray about it and talk with
strategic people. Among the five of us, who met through a coffee
house in Madison, we came up with enough money to get started
there." Berachah Farm is based on a small farm of several acres,
with one good house and three leaning buildings; it all rents for
$225, with $3500 needed for a down payment if they proceed to

buy. Robert and Marlene McGoran, twenty-one and twenty, and four others, plus three horses, some goats and chickens, inhabit 150 acres on the north shore of Shuswap Lake, as we have noted, and come back to visit JPA people in Vancouver. The Vancouver JPA crowd also has a farm at White Rock, British Columbia. A former freak, Bud Boegling, runs the House of Immanuel on fifteen acres of woods near Sumas, Washington. The chain of more than 30 Shiloh Houses launched by John Higgins near Eugene, Oregon, now has its own farm.

Jack Sparks, of the Christian World Liberation Front, explained to me why the rural trend was coming into evidence among the Jesus People. "I see it happening because it is part of the general trend. It reflects the kids' view on politics. They see city life as polluting, and they trip out to a ranch commune." Perhaps it reflects, too, a yearning of middle America, he said, and a real back-to-nature bent. And, "Kids are finding hard times getting work with their hands." He said besides the six houses backed by CWLF, the organization now has a forty-acre ranch 200 miles north of San Francisco in Garberville, California. The three couples, one single girl and seven fellows inhabit the two houses and trailer. "We feel we needed a place away from the scene, especially away from hard drugs."

The Jesus People, though their money may come from some gilded office, get a chance to rub shoulders with the factory workers and with lower and middle-class workers, both unskilled and semi-skilled. The pentecostals and Baptists, with greater strengths among the working class, are the type of churchmen the Jesus People see. There is even some growing affinity between the factory-line workers, the hard hats, and the Jesus People. I interviewed a bunch of pot-bellied, strong-armed auto factory workers in an after-hour prayer meeting in a Detroit union hall. At first I thought of "Joe" in the movie by that name about a steel worker and his hang-ups. But then I noticed that these Christian factory workers were integrated. About the long-haired Jesus People in the Detroit area, they said, "They are about the same as any other group; some of it's real, some of it isn't." And one of the men told about taking his own clean-shaven, working-class suburban down-river youth from his church to a Jesus commune to take part in a Bible study and to share testimonies, thus shoring up the faith of the straights, seeing that God can work among their long-haired peers too.

With most of the Jesus People youths involved in excessive activity and doing menial tasks, such as kitchen and latrine cleanup duty, perhaps a discipline for work is building up. I would expect to see more and more of the future communes working out creative arrangements where some youths can go to school or work outside while others stay home. Certainly Elder Ken Hollington, twenty-three, one of the four elders at Smyrna House, Toronto, is losing no talent as he does his art work (he was working on a poster commissioned at $25 by a Toronto welfare agency when I met him) and his color photography, and now, as he sets up his new electronic shop for TV repairs and other projects at the Smyrna House. Philip Shepherd, elder of Chicago's Fellowship House, is a student at the Chicago branch of the University of Illinois.

The growing ambition of members, coupled with the growing self-sufficiency of the communes to make their own way, with or without contributions, will likely make the communes and coffee houses less dependent on the businessmen, the pastors, the mission societies, the civic clubs, the radio preachers and the hucksters.

With the exploitation by older adult groups (with their traditional, personal, religious and political hang-ups) waning and failing at least in some attempts, there may likely be greater freedom for the Jesus People to develop in a counterculture that looks toward the future as well as to the past in regard to work, study and ambition.

11

Beyond Fundamentalism

Fundamentalists, like most of the rest of us, have always been involved in a certain degree of dishonesty or self-deception.

Dishonesty, how? A fundamentalist Baptist will tell you he has no creed, but put to the test he will make very clear that he adheres to a six-point creed from which there can be no divergence.

The fundamentalist plays down the idea of a formal church structure or hierarchy, emphasizing that salvation and a new life are all that matter. Nevertheless, the fundamentalists build some of the biggest churches and temples.

Most fundamentalists will swear to their last breath that they firmly support the separation of church and state and the separation of pulpit and politics. Yet a good fundamentalist preacher will allude to crime on the streets, anti-busing efforts, the militants who exceed themselves in antiwar and antidraft protests, the liberals or modernists among the main-line churches who espouse church cooperation, coexistence with the Communists. Always negative, the fundamentalists.

The fundamentalist life style is exclusive and appears to be contradictory to a loving Christ who mixed with all types. There is no allowance for fellowship with the unsaved, no allowance for joint fellowship with church youth of other persuasions, no tolerance for non-status dress patterns, no participation in the entertainment of the world—movies, theaters, etc.—no drinking and preferably no smoking, no mixing with political issues beyond denouncing public acts that go directly against the convictions of the congregation, such as anti-prayer judgments. But espousing any view that is anti-American or anti-government concerning such issues as war and peace is strictly taboo.

More self-critical are the Jesus People, and, too, more simplistic. They are too honest, too open-minded, too revolutionary and too engrossed in a part of a counterculture to be regarded as fundamentalist. The fundamentalist, like the old-line Latin-speaking Catholic, cannot get along without his tradition. Where would a fundamentalist be without his King James and Scofield Bibles, without set revival periods and programmed radio times, and without the received tradition of sixteenth century ethics and moral codes? The fundamentalist is lost without his dress code, without his Sunday-school memory verses, without the preacher to interpret the inerrant word, without his exact formulas and literal Dantean descriptions of hell. Like his main-line counterparts, the fundamentalist is also lost without his pews, his offering plates, his stained-glass windows, his church boards and the parochial ranks of deacons and superintendents, and the choir director, organist and education director.

To be sure, the Jesus People do look like fundamentalists as they carry their Bibles about, as they buttonhole you and want to know if you are saved. True, they, too, are anti-big church; they are revivalistic, liking rallies; they like lively music, co-opting modern styles as the old fundamentalists would do with their jazz-hymnists on Youth for Christ Saturday nights and Sunday evening services.

But the Jesus People cannot relate to the fundamentalist churches as such any more than they can relate to a formal Unitarian-Universalist book discussion or an Episcopalian women's afternoon card party.

Consider the basic beliefs of fundamentalists, for example, as adhered to by the conservative American Baptist Association: Their creed calls for belief in (1) the verbal inspiration of the Bible, (2) the Trinity, (3) the virgin birth, (4) the divinity of Christ, (5) the substitutionary death of Christ, (6) the bodily resurrection of Christ and the saints and the Second Coming. A group of fundamentalist Baptist national leaders put the same creedal list in somewhat different language when I queried them at one of their national conventions. But the elements were the same. And they make almost no contact with the ways of the Jesus People.

(1) The Jesus People use many versions of the Bible, for example, although book dealers tell me their Jesus People customers are heavy buyers of the American Bible Society's Good News for Modern Man. As mentioned earlier, they are often found with the Jerusalem Bible, a translation from a French ecumenical version. There is no such thing to them as a Bible-edition controversy. (2) Although the Jesus People believe in the Trinity, their concern is with the Second Person of the Trinity. With this attitude they represent what H. Richard Niebuhr (as Marty quotes him) would have called a "unitarianism of the Second Person," almost reproducing (however unconsciously) the Patripassian and Sabellian heresies of the second and third centuries. There is very little talk of the God of the Old Testament, of wrath or predestination, subjects of great concern among the fundamentalists. (3) The Jesus People do not mention the virgin birth, although they accept it. For them, Christ is all. (4) The divinity of Christ is not an issue for restatement, for Christ is real in their hearts. Formal wording gives way to the "oh wow" of experience. The Jesus People language is not the same as that of the fundamentalist creed. (5) The substitutionary death of Christ, and any other theories of the Atonement, have little meaning to the "oh wow" crowd. The trip with Christ is complete. Salvation is instant for the youths. You can find salvation with the snap of a finger, faster than a rock-ribbed fundamentalist can say "substitutionary Atonement." (6) Concerning the bodily resurrection of the saints, these youths feel thoroughly resurrected already as they live the new life. To talk of bodily resurrection later is to negate the affirmation of the bodily resurrection they know now. Often, having come through the horror of drugs, a near brush with death and OD, their bodies are suddenly alive with faith in Jesus.

While there is no great difference between the beliefs of the Jesus People and the fundamentalist creed in essence, there are substantial differences in language. And the "languages" that are spoken are what it's all about anyway, as the late William Zuurdeeg, of McCormick Theological Seminary, taught. Zuurdeeg showed how you can analyze a person's belief and faith structure by his language. Just as the neo- and logical positivists could classify language into what is meaningful and verifiable on the one hand and meaningless on the other, the Jesus People can speak in a manner that reveals their doctrine or lack of doctrine. It is the language of experience dealing with new issues. As Dr. Martin Marty notes in an article discussing theological language and the Jesus People, the choice of words betrays concepts:

> Theologians complained that few people read or understood their work; perhaps this was because both the answers and the questions to which they devoted themselves had little to do with the way people perceive the world around them.
>
> The Jesus people are trying to go beyond and behind this language and to speak in simpler, fresher ways. They stand in the tradition of the nineteenth century primitive Gospel advocates in their biblicism, though any historian of primitive Gospel movements knows that these, too, develop through history. They acquire the color of the epoch in which they appear. Therefore the current Jesus movement poses late-twentieth century issues. As this occurs, it is less important to complain about what is happening to established theological categories than it is to ask basic questions concerning the ways word and world do and should relate to each other. . . .
>
> . . . they really seem to believe that they can sustain innocence and simplicity even though no one before them has been able to, and even though the odds against them have risen today.[1]

Yet the Jesus People seem reluctant to formulate their beliefs systematically and with precision, as the fundamentalists have done. Simplicity in doctrine as in all else is the rule of their lives. It is at least possible, however, that simplicity alone may not be adequate to guarantee their continued existence and may even work against it. Thus Dr. Merne A. Harris, of the University of Iowa, insists that if the Jesus People are to persist "the Jesus People movement must define positions with reference to the following matters: (1) the inspiration of the Word of God; (2) the authority of the Word of God for human conduct in this day; (3) the mediatorial mission of Jesus Christ, (4) the ministry of the Holy Spirit, (5) the Christian ethic, and (6) the question of eschatology. To date I have had no facet of this movement answer these questions satisfactorily and for this reason I consider the Jesus People movement a shallow, superficial expression of religious life."

But cataloguing theological fine points does not create criteria for what is true and valid. If Harris is correct, then poetry is less valid and less useful than a bill of sale or legal document of transfer of real estate. Preciseness may serve to hasten the day of institutionalism of the movement, but the movement can exist—and probably can do so in its most influential form—without categorization, at least *pro tem*. For there is a certain wisdom of the Jesus People in their alienation when they avoid becoming set in formulations like those of fundamentalism. And this is true even though the formalizing process is going on, as we have seen in the case of the Children of God, who already have taken on many of the characteristics of a denomination, and of other groups, too, who, contrary to the Children of God, take part in such federated activities as joint rallies and conventions.

David Burrell, C.S.C., who works with alternative life styles at Notre Dame, stresses that the key role of the Jesus People and many of the various mystical groups consists of more than asserting old beliefs or launching comparable beliefs. To regard the Jesus People and similar movements as fundamentalism is to reflect not only one's own prior hang-ups and limited frames of reference but to assert a hidden death wish for the movement. Inherent at least is a wish that the Jesus People will go away or hide behind some rock and leave the rest of humanity, including the organized church institutions, alone. Father Burrell says:

. . . references to "a new fundamentalism," or . . . to a "new religious phenomenon" is our characteristic way of at once reporting what is happening and of writing it off as yet something else to be viewed, catalogued and forgotten. . . .

To label this "a new fundamentalism" or to regard it as a "phenomenon" is to overlook the intense desire to come close to themselves and their God which motivates these young people. For we have succeeded in turning their quest and their lives into an abstraction by the simple application of a label. . . .

What we are encountering in groups such as these is a compelling desire for simplicity, directness and candor. To describe this as a form of *fundamentalism* is to place a superfluous screen between what is going on and those who wish to understand it. For fundamentalism describes a doctrinal and moral posture assumed by people who have much to lose if certain fundaments of their position were removed. Hence they had a great deal at stake in defending a word-by-word inspiration of the Bible. These young people, however, are not concerned about defending anything. They are rather enthusiastic about what they have discovered once they have broken through multiple academic screens to simply reading their Scriptures. However this attitude may differ from case to case, I'm confident that in many of them it represents a hard-won simplicity. That means that the critical and theological obstacle course has in one way or another been passed through.[2]

I

While the fundamentalists and evangelicals (moderate fundamentalists with some social concern) are having difficulty faulting the Jesus People movement, they discuss it with guarded feelings and are quick to warn of potential (if not presently existing) problems in the movement. Thus the Rev. Hudson T. Armeding, president of the National Association of Evangelicals, said in a Los Angeles speech that there is "the danger of faddism that too often is the product of an incomplete view of the person and work of Christ." In a Los Angeles *Times* interview he elaborated: "The Jesus People we have had contact with seem to have a high view of Scripture and Christ, as we do, but they should be careful that it is not hurt by people who are attracted to it because it's exciting and different," a danger, he said, in all religious movements.[3]

The evangelical can accept the Jesus People on his own terms, at best, or at worst hold up a question mark and keep them at a distance. On the opposite side, the Rev. James Spillman, thirty-six, minister of education, Calvary (Baptist) Temple, Denver, Colorado, tenth largest Protestant church in the U.S. with 9,500 members, notes, "The Jesus People movement can contribute to the 'bridge' that is missing between the institutional church and the 'lost' generation. The Jesus People are an addition to the ministry of Christ that is at once sensational, but perplexing, in that each one does 'that which is right in his own eyes.' This leads to many kinds of behavior and strange attitudes." He maintains that the

Jesus People should not be incorporated into regular church life, for "the fresh breath of air that their ministry has would be stifled."

On the more reserved side, the Rev. Warren Benson, forty-one, central regional director, Gospel Light Publications, Wheaton, Illinois, notes that the Jesus People's "impact will be negligible in their terms on the institutional church because of their obvious disenchantment of it and conversely the institutional church's with them." And: "I am afraid that the evangelical church is too frozen and wooden to accept the Jesus People." The Rev. Mel Johnson, fifty-two, of Minneapolis, director of a radio program, Tips for Teens, noted, "They may be inadequate in their lack of knowledge to balance with their zeal." And he believes there has to be some appreciation of the "purpose of the church" before there is any meaningful relationship between the Jesus People and the church, and vice versa.

It is at this point of the "church" that the real fundamentalists (those who like to be called fundamentalists) definitely square off at the Jesus People. Other things, however, are cited, too. Consider these statements to me from leading fundamentalist leaders in the U.S. and Canada at a Fundamentalist Baptist convention:

Dr. Joseph M. Stowell, Des Plaines, Illinois, chief executive officer of the General Association of Regular Baptist Churches, an organization of 1,500 churches:

"No doubt some of the so-called Jesus People are truly saved. We rejoice in this. We decry the movement's apparent rejection of the spiritual teaching on the local New Testament church. Also we believe strongly in the divine institution of the family and regret to hear of some Jesus People living in communes. Any movement ignoring these two matters cannot survive as a Christian movement."

Dr. H. C. Slade, Jarvis Street Baptist Church, Toronto, Ontario, Canada, president of Toronto Baptist Seminary and editor of *Gospel Witness:*

"The Jesus People disregard the church, and although some talk evangelical and about being born again, they are also inadequate concerning the atonement and their lack of emphasis on it."

Dr. Monroe Parker, Decatur, Alabama, full-time evangelist, general director of the Baptist World Mission, former president of the Pillsbury Baptist Bible College, Owatonna, Minnesota, and former president of the Minnesota Baptist Convention:

"While many of the so-called Jesus People have had a personal encounter with Jesus Christ, their leaders are very unwise in encouraging them to remain outside of the organized churches. Jesus founded a church at Jerusalem which ought to be the prototype of all other churches. The New Testament knows nothing of a churchless Christianity."

Dr. H. Frank Collins, pastor of the 2,200 member Calvary Baptist Church, Bellflower, California, and president of the six-state Baptist Bible Fellowship:

"They are fundamental on salvation and the second coming of Christ. They are *not* fundamentalists on the doctrine of the authority of the church and all authority as set forth. In California, where I am, their effort has been *always* detrimental to the established church (which for 1,900 years has propagated the gospel of Christ and to which they owe whatever knowledge they have). Evangelistic and enthusiastic, yes! Profitable? Drug addicts find escape here. Certainly profitable here! But enduring and profitable to the eternal cause of Christ? No! Women may give birth to children in the desert, but the responsibility of the ensuing years is another question. Same principle!"

The Rev. John Rawlings, fifty-seven, twenty-year pastor of the Landmark Baptist Temple, Cincinnati, Ohio, and vice president of the Baptist Bible College, Springfield, Missouri:

"The Jesus People are products of liberal and old-time apostasy. These young people are empty but sincere in their seeking. It would be wrong blatantly to condemn them. Their apostasy is moral as well as spiritual. They have no absolutes. They are like a ship without a rudder. They need the truth, a fence to keep some things in and some things out. They must have standards of spiritual enlightenment and also concerning parental authority. In their beliefs, they stray from the Word of God in departing from the authority of the local church (I Tim. 3:15, 'Thou oughtest to behave thyself in the house of God, which is the church of the living God, the pillar and ground of the truth')."

The Rev. J. Don Jennings, thirty-nine, pastor, Calvary Baptist

Church, Ypsilanti, Michigan, secretary, Fundamental Baptist Congress of North America:

"Jesus People are not fundamentalists! The true meaning of 'fundamental' is 'a belief in the basic tenets of the Bible.' The Bible is not a heavenly cafeteria from which we pick and choose what we want or do not want. Well meaning young people choose the Jesus image but do not live the Jesus life! Ornamental cross wearing is more popular than sacrificial cross bearing. Jesus said, 'Not everyone that saith Lord, Lord, shall enter into the kingdom of heaven.' They are long on zeal but short on Biblical knowledge."

II

In the area of personal habits, the Jesus People are not of one stripe like the fundamentalists. The Jesus People do not worry about smoking or drinking. Occasionally in some of the houses you see even the girls light up a cigarette. They stick by the Scriptures, which do not mention cigarettes and which do not explicitly condemn alcohol. Thus they will and do use wine at communion in many places. Socially, the Fellowship House in Chicago permits a little beer with pizza on Saturday night during the TV movies. Recording rock-folk singer Ken Christie, who works a northwest Detroit lounge six nights a week, does not regard himself as one of the Jesus People. Yet he conducts his own Bible rap, speaks of Jesus in the club, performs in churches with his long-haired group on Sundays and also passes out the Hollywood *Free Paper* in Flint, where he lives. He'll buy you and your friends a drink sometimes as he raps about the faith with you, nursing what looks like a Manhattan and puffing on a cigarette. "The church tries to dictate righteousness or program people this way or that, but you can't do that," he says. "There's no Scripture against social drinking, no Scripture against smoking, just religious dogma."

Both controversial liberal theologians Martin Marty, of the University of Chicago, and Harvey Cox, of Harvard Divinity School, are "turned on" by facets of the Jesus People movement, even though they may not agree on an appreciation of the role of the Jesus People in history (with Cox they are a part of a bigger force shaping the future; with Marty, it's wait and see and a doubt that they can survive the overexposure in media and fast acceleration of the times).

Marty notes an affinity of the Jesus People with past liberals of history, both experientially and rationally:

Their (the young people's) approach, despite the superficial and external accommodations to evangelical orthodoxy, actually includes elements congenial to the heirs of nineteenth century liberalism. One strand, deriving from the whole Schleiermacherian century's accent on experience, warms to their love of personal experience (which is not only the evangelical's accent), and the freaks are water on parched ground wherever liberalism forgot that and turned merely intellectual. "Big liberal churches" around America are experience-hungry. And the freaks' Jesus has much in common with the liberals' Jesus, the gentle poet of the Galilean hills, who can be appropriated without the accretions of centuries of dogma.[4]

Cox, who found quick identification with Jesus People who came to interrupt his lecture at the University of Houston, told of his experience and confrontation with the Jesus youth: "The administrative officers were embarrassed, but I said, 'marvelous.' " The youths began singing. Cox asked them: "Can I sing with you?"

Cox, who grew up as a Baptist and can sing stanzas of "Amazing Grace," Judy Collins never heard of, said he then told the youths: "Would you read my favorite passages?"

And they did. "They didn't mind reading any parts of the Bible. They were not real fundamentalists, for many fundamentalists are suspicious of parts of the Bible. Most fundamentalists say about the Sermon on the Mount (verses preoccupied with loving one another, instead of doctrine) that it belongs to some different dispensation of time and does not rank as high as other Scriptures."

Even if the movement were decidedly fundamentalist, the Jesus People and fundamentalism would not coexist for long. Says Dr. George M. Alexander, dean of the School of Theology, University of the South, at Sewanee, Tennessee: "The fundamentalist basis for the movement is in time likely to prove unacceptable to sharp-minded young people. People seeking Jesus only for their own personal motives, not to be parts of his mission, tend soon to fall away. Lack of background might just produce false fruits."

Dr. Eugene Carson Blake, of the World Council of Churches, tells me, "If the theology behind the movement continues to be as fundamentalist and unsophisticated as some of the adult leaders would make it out to be, it will doubtless pass very quickly. There are indications that the young people themselves have much better theological insight than some of the adult leaders who started it or who have more recently got on the band wagon."

Some of the young critics of the movement believe that the Jesus People are "a set-up for the Billy Graham movement," as Howard Horvath, twenty-three, a Methodist campus minister at the Illinois Institute of Technology, put it. Most of the Jesus People have little quarrel with Graham, but they do not say much about him, either. Some will send delegations to his meetings. But the only personality they seem excited about is Kathryn Kuhlman, for whom a whole house of Jesus People will stand in line three hours early to be sure of seats. Her emphasis is on the healing of the Spirit. The movement is heavy into the Spirit, if not healing as such, and so the imaginations of young Jesus People are captured more quickly by her approach than by that of a shouting Baptist. Graham also comes off very straight to some of them. And he is a symbol of death for the movement to others. "The death of Christianity has always been tied in with Christian synthesis (of the world and faith)," said Philip Shepherd, a University of Illinois student and elder of the Fellowship House, Chicago. "Graham is a beautiful example of this synthesis, with his $300 suits and his arm around Nixon.

"Jesus People will have to get more involved in culture. There is no way out. The Jesus People should not put their heads in the sand during a storm, but in a storm, nail up the shutters. If they are children of light, how can they be afraid of reality?"

III

The future of the movement, on its given premises, will evolve in two directions, and in both of them farther and farther from a fundamentalist churchly concept, Philip Shepherd believes. He says (1) there will either be more individualism and a growing monasticism, or (2) a move to be involved in society, and "not just in social services," which could very likely include the political arena.

Shepherd continued, "The early Christians were political. They confronted the power structure—the Sadducees, the Pharisees, the Romans. It is a whole history of God 'doing'—an unfolding. The early Christians were spreading a new message. Christ was also the answer for culture."

Because the world is basically humanist, it needs an alternative, Shepherd says. Extremist views on the right and left, he believes, "are two forms of the same dilemma of humanism. Humanism also begins with the idea that man is captain of his own ship." Shepherd, whose dad is a deacon in a Wilmette Lutheran church and vice president of an insurance company, says Christians and the revolutionary-minded Jesus People can bring an alternative. "Christians will realize they are the real radicals." He believes the Jesus People movement might develop toward Christian parties, possibly with names such as Christian Liberation Party or Christian Free Party. He cited examples of former Christian unionism experiments in the United States and one, the Christian Labour Association of Canada, headquartered in Rexdale, Ontario, that is now successful.

It was almost a political move in 1971 when Jesus People outside the General Assembly meeting of the United Presbyterians in Buffalo dubbed themselves the United Presbyterian Liberation Front, so that they could lobby effectively for a "personal experience with Christ" to the delegates.

The Christian World Federation Front, in Berkeley, took its political cue from the campus radicals. The group sought to preach in the same locations, even evangelize among the same crowds. And the tabloid newspapers—more than 100 of them—are a copy of CWLF underground format, a copy itself of the underground newssheets. As the counterculture youths grow older and if they step up their activity in other areas, they—the Jesus People movement included—might well indeed enter the political arena. Asked if he would run for office someday, Shepherd said "far-out," but later?—"when a little older."

It is possible, as eighteen-year-olds are allowed to vote, that politics might take on new interest for the young, including the Jesus People. They believe in short routes, and some like Tippit in Chicago and Blessitt of Los Angeles, New York, and Belfast, like to do battle in the public arena. Increasingly it might dawn on

them that the politics of silence is not necessarily the best steward-
ship of God's gifts to them, and if social concern grows (as we
noted), then the additional power means for achieving them most
efficiently might come under consideration.

The future of the Jesus People movement was never in a fundamentalist camp to begin with. The dynamics are too diverse. They
could never accept the single-minded narrowness of the conservatives.

I see the Jesus movement going in five directions, any one or all
of which could have its impact on the future of society and religion:

—The Children of God seem well on the way to becoming a
formal denomination with missions overseas, conventions, central
financing, etc. This is a route that may well be taken by others in
the movement.

—Main-line denominations will absorb some of the new Jesus
youth. This is being done already as youth directors set up coffee
houses and work on dialogue with the Jesus youth to get them into
the churches. The success of Evangelist Richard Hogue in the
South and the success of Calvary Chapel, Costa Mesa, California,
with its pew-sitting freak crowd, indicate growing assimilation. Institutional men such as Eugene Carson Blake, of the World Council
of Churches; positive thinker Norman Vincent Peale; and Catholic
Bishop Fulton Sheen underscore the adult acceptance of Jesus
People, which is a part of assimilation, as these leaders congratu-
late the Jesus People for their dedication and enthusiasm.

—Some men of charisma might develop a guru or maharishi
relationship with pockets of the youth, as personality cults develop (as Mr. George Aichele is quoted predicting earlier in this
book), transitional in the long run to something else.

—There might be room for some terror, nonreligious groups
coming out of the hypnotic Children of God, if Cindy (in the account of the group in Detroit) is right. As eclecticism and the
broadening of faiths continue, the emphasis on the occult in some
parts of the movement may develop into magical, semi-Christian
mystical cults.

—I see also the mainstream of the Jesus People continuing.
Possibly, with the revolutionary prodding, something big and new
might emerge, *e.g.,* a churchless, celebrative religion, with both

liberal and conservative wings, riding the tide of the general unrest as a new "consciousness" is being created. It is even possible that they may bring renewal and rebirth to a pale, tired, dry, churchly Christianity.

Chris Meyer, twenty-two, a Quaker, who works in non-violent training and organizing in peace education for the American Friends Service Committee, raps the glut of words of the Jesus People movement. He calls this talkativeness a "politics of mysticism, a belief that talking about the gospel does it." Words without application. "We call it rhetoric in the movement," he said.

"I do not say the Jesus People are dangerous." And: "Something in them will die in five years."

Something will live, too.

Maybe something much more—less tangible, but tangible enough to be capable of evaluation and tracking by a later historian.

Something like the contributions of insignificant saints, and great ones, too, such as martyred Polycarp at the stake in the second century; the Eastern formulators of faith of the fourth—Basil of Caesarea, Gregory of Nyssa, and Gregory of Nazianzus; the humble reformer Francis; forceful, dynamic crusaders such as Dominic and Bernard of Clairvaux of the Middle Ages; and the revivalists (many of whose followers left legacies of structures) of the eighteenth and nineteenth centuries, not all of them perfect but most of them used by God.

These men—many of them in time called saints—were not buzzed. They were not rubbed out, in history, by even the greatest array of contemporary assessment—and action—against them. Their names—and their gifts—remain.

Other names and callings may remain, too.

Oh, wow, Jesus. . . .

Notes

CHAPTER 1

1. Kieran Quinn, "What Do You Say to a Jesus Freak?", *The Critic,* September–October, 1971, Vol. XXX, no. 1, p. 64.

CHAPTER 2

1. Donald E. Mullen, "Campus Crusade for Christ Aims Its Gospel at the Young," *United Press International,* June 20, 1971.
2. Nathan Adler, "Hippies Are New-Time Gnostics," *Christian Advocate,* March 4, 1971, p. 3.
3. Rev. Father I. J. Mikulski, *Question Box,* "Jesus People Sound Groovy," *The Catholic Weekly,* May 7, 1971, p. 4.
4. Williston Walker, *A History of the Christian Church* (New York: Charles Scribner's Sons, 1950), p. 504.
5. *Ibid.,* p. 505.
6. *Ibid.,* p. 510.
7. *Viewpoint,* editorial, "The Jesus Revolution," *Together,* August–September, 1971, p. 22.
8. "Jesus Explosion" (Part II), *Home Missions,* August, 1971, Vol. XLII, no. 8, p. 29; "A Good Sound," letter by John R. Sampey III.
9. Charles A. Reich, *The Greening of America* (New York: Bantam Books, 1971), p. 287.
10. Theodore Roszak, *The Making of a Counterculture* (Garden City, N.Y.: Anchor Books, Doubleday & Co., Inc., 1969), p. 40.
11. *Communal Forms: Emergent Power Bases: Implications for Church and Society,* The Reflections of Dietrich Bonhoeffer House, University of Chicago, compiled by Carl D. Onofrio, pp. 79, 80. Mimeographed, n.d.
12. Robert Lynn and Elliott Wright, *The Big Little School* (New York: Harper and Row, 1971.)

CHAPTER 3

1. Duane Pederson, *Jesus People* (Pasadena, Calif.: Compass Press, 1971), p. 83.
2. *Ibid.*, p. 84.
3. David Wilkerson, *The Cross and the Switchblade* (New York: Bernard Geis Associates, 1963), p. 165.
4. Lon F. Backman, "Linda's Revolutionary Army," *World Vision Magazine*, July–August, 1970, p. 14.
5. Ed Plowman, "Pacific Northwest: Revival in the 'Underground'," *Christianity Today*, Jan. 29, 1971, p. 35.
6. Donald M. Williams, "Close-up of the Jesus People," *Christianity Today*, August 27, 1971, p. 5.
7. George Cornell, "Religion Today," *Associated Press Newsfeatures*, New York, March 19, 1971.
8. Editorial, "The Jesus Revolution," *Together Magazine*, Aug.–Sept., 1971, p. 22.

CHAPTER 4

1. Cf. "Where Have All the Children Gone?", special report, *Christianity Today*, Nov. 5, 1971, Vol. XVI, no. 3, p. 38.

CHAPTER 5

1. Earl C. Gottschalk, Jr., "The Jesus People Are Coming," *The Lutheran*, May 5, 1971, p. 12, a reprint from *The Wall Street Journal*, March 2, 1971, "Hip Culture Discovers a New High: Fervent, Foot-Stomping Religion," p. 14.
2. "Young Evangelist's First Target Here Is a Times Square Bookstore Specializing in the Erotic," New York *Times*, June 7, 1970, p. 45.

CHAPTER 7

1. Andrew Greeley, "The Sacred and the Psychedelic," *The Critic*, April–May, 1969, p. 30.
2. *Ibid.*

CHAPTER 8

1. Hal Lindsey with C. C. Carlson, *The Late Great Planet Earth* (Grand Rapids, Mich.: Zondervan, 1970), pp. 112, 113.
2. Gabriel Fackre, "Going East: Neomysticism and Christian Faith," *Christian Century*, April 14, 1971, p. 458.
3. Martin Marty, "Doing the Jesus Thing," in *Context*, April 1, 1971, reprinted in *Home Missions*, September, 1971, Vol. 42, no. 9, p. 35.
4. Levi H. Dowling, *The Aquarian Gospel of Jesus the Christ* (Santa Monica: Calif.: DeVorss & Co., © Leo W. Dowling, 1964, introduction, Eva S. Dowling).

5. *Ibid.,* p. 17.
6. John Dart, "Supernatural Found Central to Communes," Los Angeles *Times,* Nov. 8, 1970, Section E, p. 18.
7. Jacob Needleman, "Winds From the East; Youths and Counter-cults," *Commonweal,* April 30, 1971, Vol. xciv, no. 8, p. 189.
8. *Ibid.*
9. *Ibid.*
10. John Groutt, "Communes: A Revolutionary Alternative to Institutional Religion," in Elwyn A. Smith, ed., *What the Religious Revolutionaries Are Saying* (Philadelphia: Fortress Press, 1971), p. 109.

CHAPTER 9

1. *Principles of Church Union,* Consultation on Church Union, adopted 1966 (Cincinnati: Forward Movement Publications, 1966), p. 35.
2. "Life in a Jesus People Commune Is Crowded but Scriptural," Kitchener-Waterloo (Ontario) *Record,* July 24, 1971.

CHAPTER 10

1. *Christianity Today,* June 18, 1971, p. 36.
2. Phil Tracy, "The Jesus Freaks," *Commonweal,* Vol. XLIII, no. 5, p. 124.
3. James Nolan, "Jesus Now: Hogwash and Holy Water," *Ramparts,* August, 1971, Vol. 10, no. 2, p. 26.

CHAPTER 11

1. Martin E. Marty, "Jesus: The Media and the Message," *Theology Today,* Vol. XXVIII, no. 4, January 1972, pp. 474, 475.
2. David Burrell, *Ave Maria,* January 10, 1970, Vol. III, number 2, p. 10.
3. John Dart, "Evangelist Worried by New Interest in Jesus," Los Angeles *Times,* April 2, 1971, p. 18.
4. Martin Marty, "Doing the Jesus Thing," in *Context,* April 1, 1971, reprinted in *Home Missions,* September, 1971, Vol. 42, no. 9, p. 35.

Appendixes

A. Rules of Jesus Communes

In some of the Jesus People houses, rules are posted. In others, they are merely understood. In still others there are fragments, little warnings or directions scattered about on a bulletin board, on parts of the kitchen walls, on bathroom doors. These go from the sublime to the ridiculous. Sublime are the general guidelines spoken orally by leaders of the Fellowship House:—"No premarital sex, no drugs, do your job, continue personal relationship with Christ, come to Bible study—this is not just a dorm." Ridiculous it would seem are the Children of God little directives in the bathroom. Above the toilet paper, they write: "Two sheets—three in emergency: Proverbs 30:7" (the verse when you look it up says: "Two things have I required of thee; deny me them not before I die" followed by verse 8 which says: "Remove far from me vanity . . .")

Here are samplings of several Jesus House lists of rules as they are posted for members.

SHEEPFOLD HOUSE, MILWAUKEE, WIS.

Daily

7 A.M.	—	Cook up, starts breakfast; others, quiet devotions.
8	—	All up.
8:30	—	Prayer downstairs.
9	—	Breakfast.
9:30	—	Chores.

10	—	Bible study downstairs.
11:30	—	Lunch—snack; crews to streets, coffee house, office.
5 P.M.	—	Cook in.
6:30	—	Dinner.
8	—	Bible study—coffee house or back to street.

Saturday

8 A.M.	—	Cook up.
9	—	All up.
11	—	Bible study at coffee house.
12 N.	—	Peanut butter snack—on street.
8:30 P.M.	—	Coffee house.

Sunday

Individual rising, breakfast and clean-up. To churches for those going.

2:30 P.M.	—	Coffee-house service of prayer, elders serving.
5:30	—	Dinner—only meal prepared.
7:30	—	Separate Bible study, men and women.

Consideration for the brethren: Quiet before rising hour, after 11 P.M. keep music pleasing to God. See elders about overnight guests. Dress to come downstairs. Fellows and girls meet downstairs, not in rooms. Keep your own room neat—clean up after yourself. Use bath on your floor; pick up after yourself. Be responsible for chores assigned. Let your elder know where you are at all times. Smoking guests use porch. Use pay phone for personal calls.

Praise the Lord in all things!

EMMAUS HOUSE, TORONTO, CAN.

JESUS SAID, "YOU MUST LOVE THE LORD YOUR GOD WITH ALL YOUR HEART, ALL YOUR SOUL, AND WITH ALL YOUR MIND." THIS IS THE GREATEST AND THE FIRST COMMANDMENT. THE SECOND IS LIKE IT: "YOU MUST LOVE YOUR NEIGHBOUR AS YOURSELF. ON THESE TWO COMMANDMENTS HANG THE WHOLE LAW, AND THE PROPHETS ALSO."
(MATTHEW 22:37)

The members of this community live by the above words of Jesus. In order to carry them out effectively in day-to-day living, the members of the House of Emmaus are accepting the following rules, and the full authority of the Elder as defined in the Scriptures.

1. Anyone wishing to stay up after midnight must be quiet so as not to disturb those who are in bed. No talking is allowed after 12:30 A.M.

2. Beds must be made every morning.

3. Personal belongings should be kept in bedrooms, bathroom, basement or workshop; not in the kitchen, halls, or living room.

4. There will be no smoking in the house.

5. Secular literature is not to be left in the public areas of the house. Only Christian music is permitted.

6. Lunch will be served at 12 noon and supper at 6 P.M.

7. Only foods so designated will be used for snacks.

8. Anyone eating or having coffee or tea on his own must wash, dry and put away their dishes and clean up after themselves.

9. Permission must be received from Tom if for any reason a resident cannot attend the house meetings or participate in other activities of the house.

10. Permission must be obtained from the Elder if a resident wishes to leave the community for more than 24 hours.

11. A visitor who wishes to stay overnight must receive permission from Tom.

12. A person may join the community permanently by a decision of the Elder in consultation with the residents of the house.

13. It is everyone's responsibility to help with the financial upkeep of the house. A contribution of $2.00 per day must be made by every resident. This must be paid in advance unless special arrangements are made with the Elder.

SMYRNA HOUSE, WESTON, ONTARIO, CAN.

RULES AND REGULATIONS

1. All people must be up and out of bed *by* 9:00 A.M.

2. Guests shall be out *by* 12:00 midnight.

3. All residing people shall be in bed no later than 1:00 A.M.

4. Supper shall be served at 6:00 P.M. If not the house people shall fast.

5. Breakfast shall be served at 10:00 A.M.

6. There shall be one inside workday per week, work and day designated by Lyn H.

7. There shall be *no one* who lives in this house who smokes.

8. There shall be one outside workday per week, work and day designated by Rich Howard.

9. There shall be no smoking in the house except in the middle meeting room and the coffee shop.

10. Smoking prohibited in the coffee shop on Sat. nights.

11. All house people *shall* be at the meetings held by the house and should be at the other meetings at the house.

12. All house people shall attend the Bible study and prayer held after each supper meal.

13. Only house persons shall be permitted in the *upstairs, office areas* and *kitchen;* any other persons by permission of house persons.

14. Only music of a Christian nature shall be permitted by the house people on the main floor.

15. Any house person shall notify the body in case of absence from meals and for accommodations.

Any other rules or guidelines shall come from the Scripture, therefore we must study the Scripture daily to be approved of God and each other.

All complaints and/or general family discussions is to be mentioned at the supper meal.

In all things let us strive and pray for the unity of the Body of Christ.

> "Do all you can to preserve
> the unity of the Spirit . . ."
> (Eph. 4:3)

YOUTH FOR TRUTH, SACRAMENTO, CALIF.

When you get up in the morning, you are expected to clean up your personal area, make your bed, clean and lock your locker, and take care of your own hygiene. The ministry provides mouthwash, toothpaste, deodorant, razor blades, haircuts and plenty of soap. Take advantage of these and you will become a real blessing to yourself and to your brothers and sisters. If we feel that you are failing to give adequate care to any of these areas, you may be sure that it will be brought to your attention and you will be expected to take care of it.

Whenever you use anything, be sure it goes back where it belongs, whether it be clothes, toiletries, dishes, newspapers, books, towels, paper, chairs, etc. Each person must do his share if this ministry is to function in an organized and orderly fashion.

Let's Be Considerate

We must all be sensitive to the needs and tastes of the 20-plus people who are living in the same house. Unnecessary stomping, yelling, screaming and general carrying-on are prohibited and do not contribute to the quiet spiritual atmosphere. Walk softly and learn to be a quiet person. Foolish jesting, joking, horseplay can be dangerous and cause unnecessary friction. This does not mean that you must walk around with a long face all the time, but be sure that your joy and happiness are unto the Lord.

Ladies and Gentlemen

This is a Christian house and you will act like Christian ladies and gentlemen, not only in your dress, but in your manners and actions. Let your conversation be edifying to the Lord and try to use good table manners. If you don't know how to be mannerly, you will be taught. It is our house policy to have all guests served first, then the young ladies and then the gentlemen. Gentlemen—try opening doors for the girls, seating them at the table and just generally giving them the courtesy and respect that they need. Tell each other how much you appreciate one another and remember Christian Love is different than that which you have known in the world. We try and help you overcome any temptation in that area by traveling in separate vehicles and limiting physical contact to hand shaking. If you find yourself "falling in love," go to your counselor and get it out in the open. Pray that God will show you His direct will for you in this area; marriages made by man are not happy or lasting.

Special House Rules and Regulations

We here at YFTC stand assured and fully convinced of the importance of discipline in the Christian walk. We do not feel that the regulations and standards set forth in the above and the following pages are too difficult to follow if you are truly interested in getting yourself together. Scripture tells us to give correction three times and then cast the offender out. We do, however, understand how difficult it is for someone off the streets to come into this situation and conform. Therefore we will call you before the Inner Board if you must be corrected more than twice for the same offense, and they will decide whether or not you should be reprimanded, given special duties or asked to leave the center.

House Meetings and Activities

House meetings are held every other Thursday and everyone in the house is required to attend. This is a time we get together and share any problems we are having, any blessings that the Lord has done for us, or decide on any house policies, etc. Come prepared to contribute, constructively criticize, share and participate. Saturday and Tuesday nights are recreation time. Saturdays we will be going on various outings and picnics and Tuesdays we will be having recreation and exercise. We have engagements, functions, etc., that you must attend if you are able. Come prepared, so that the meetings can run without interruption for such things as drinks of water and trips to the restroom.

On Time
Always be on time for all meetings, activities, functions, and meals. Everyone will get up at the appointed time and lights will go out at 10:00 P.M. each week night. Continued tardiness will justify an Inner Board ruling.

Meals
We have two meals a day (three on special occasions) and piece-mealing (snacking) is prohibited, unless special permission is given by a supervisor. This includes coffee, candy bars, potato chips, etc. It isn't fair or polite for you to eat in front of others unless there is enough for all, besides, it gets to be a mess.

Everyone will eat all scheduled meals unless you are on the fast list, or sick, or on a special errand. There are two bells for the meals—the first is a five-minute warning bell to give you a chance to wash up and finish what you are doing, and the second is for grace. If you are not present for grace you will be considered not eating. We are thankful for the food that the Lord has provided for this ministry and we eat very well. If there is something served that you are not fond of, please keep your comments to yourself, or bring them before the Lord.

Off Limits
Because of health regulations, fire hazards, and personal safety, there are limitations on certain areas of the house. The attic is completely off limits unless permission is granted from a supervisor for printing or getting donations. The kitchen is also off limits except for the cooks, dishwashers and table-setters. Guests are limited to the living room, chapel and dining area, unless they are being shown the house. The "Dorm" is off limits from after breakfast until dinner except for prayer. Don't let this become a place of escape. The office is off limits to everyone except the secretaries, Harold, Gene and those with official business.

Office

The office is for business, not social activities. Please keep out unless you have definite business there. It opens at 9:00 A.M. and closes at 4:00 P.M., so please conduct any business that you have during this time. Office materials and machines are not property of anyone in the center. Please ask permission to use any of the machines, equipment or supplies. You may have two stamps a week for your personal letters. Please be considerate and respect the privacy of the office. When the door is shut . . . *don't even knock,* unless it is an emergency. It is closed for a reason and unwanted interruption is one of them.

Work Details

We are all part of this family and must all do what is expected of us in order for things to be run decently and in order. Check with the supervisor or counselor and find out what is your duty for the week. A detail list will be posted weekly, so please be sure that the job given you is done efficiently and quickly. Remember that the Lord sees all that we do and he rewards you for being conscientious and obedient. Sickness is the only legitimate excuse for not completing your duties.

Showers and Laundry

Baths and showers may be taken with permission during the daily free time or from 6:30 to 9:30 at night. You will be issued two towels a week so take care of them and leave the bath area as clean as you found it.

CHILDREN OF GOD, WOODLAND PARK, COLO.

9 A.M.	—	Ten-minute "inspirational singing." Classes.
11	—	Breakfast (cereal, sausage, pancakes, toast, fruit).
12 noon	—	Work. Girls prepare meals, care for babies, clean. Guys: Wash dishes, fix cars, work outdoors on ranch.
Afternoon	—	Two hours free time; a class, and songs.
6 P.M.	—	Dinner (salad, stew, "or something. You always get potato and meat, and rice").
Evening	—	Inspiration (music), study, witnessing.

(From a Children of God communication)

The Rules of the Revolution are strict: Attend all classes and meetings, study and go witnessing, do your duties faithfully, arise when wakened and retire at lights out. Study to be quiet and "to show thyself approved unto God, a workman that needeth not to be ashamed, rightly dividing the word of Truth." "Preach the Word, be instant in season and out," and "always ready to give an answer to him that asketh thee." "Let everything be done decently and in order, for God is not the author of confusion"—keep your quarters neat and tidy and yourself clean. "Defile not the temple of the Holy Ghost"—no smoking or smooching other than "greeting one another with a holy kiss"—and absolutely no dating. Betrothals only for staff members after months of service and ready to go on their own with Team approval. Do not leave anywhere without permission and absence from Bible study, duties or witnessing must be only for emergencies by direct permission of the officer in charge. Absence without leave will be considered desertion of your post. You will only be given one warning, after which your place will be given some-one more deserving. "He sent them out two by two"—you will never go alone, and always a veteran with trainee.

The Hours of Revolution are strenuous, and vary with each local battle conditions. Since much of our work is done at night, usually to very late hours, sometimes all night in meetings, witnessing, etc., your mornings are generally your own for prayer and Bible study and personal duties, with "brunch" in the late morning (no lunch), class or witnessing in the afternoon, dinner at 6, meetings or witnessing at night, sometimes a night snack or refreshments, and quietly to bed. Unusual circumstances or assignments can change this at a moment's notice, without complaint. The only things you can be sure of are the Lord, hard work, suffering, constant change and joy. There are no days off, except some Saturdays or special days, and that usually without meals.

The Behavior of the Revolutionary is quiet, orderly, obedient, cheerful, willing, and faithful as well as diligent, respectful, sacrificial and long-suffering, meek, gentle, peaceful, loving, unselfish and kind, "forgiving one another, as God for Christ's sake hath forgiven you." "Above all else, having fervent love one toward another." All must memorize and practice I Cor. 13. In the field, instant obedience is imperative, with the welfare and safety of souls and your fellows at stake. Obey the laws and officers of the law, owners of property and officials of schools or estab-lishments. "Agree with thine adversary whilst thou art in the way with him, lest he hail thee to the officer, and he take thee before the judge, who shall cast thee into jail, and thou shalt not come forth from thence till thou hast paid the last farthing!"—Jesus' own warning! "If they re-fuse to receive thee, shake off the dust of thy feet and depart." "If they persecute you in one city, flee to another." Don't stop to argue! We don't put up bail or wait for court trials. "Be all things to all men in order that you might win some"—be winsome!

The Equipment, Uniform and Appearance of a Revolutionary depend largely on the field of battle. "To the Jew as a Jew, the Greek as a Greek, the Roman as a Roman"—or the hippie as a hippie! While with a type of people, you adopt the costume and customs of your mission field, with rare exceptions. Jesus adopted the flesh of sinful man, "that we through his poverty might become rich." "Let us therefore follow after the things which make for peace. . . . For meat destroy not the work of God. . . . It is good neither to do anything whereby thy brother stumbleth or is offended. If every one of us please his neighbor." So you will change according to field conditions—on order if necessary—"without strife or vain disputation." Informal sport clothing is generally acceptable for most conditions, without extremes, *except for special occasions as ordered.* One small suitcase or bag, two or three inches of hang-up clothes, Bible, notebook and pen, with one coat and your bed-roll. Cameras, tape recorders, radios and music instruments are very useful.

The Discipline of Jesus' Revolutionaries must be absolute "obedience to them that have the rule over them, for they care for their souls, as they that must themselves give account." "Whatsoever thy hand findeth to do, do it with thy might" "as unto the Lord, and not unto man," "all for the glory of God," for "they that shall not work, shall not eat"—duties, study, witnessing, sharing, prayer, praising, sacrificing, suffering, persecution and even martyrdom! You must obey implicitly, quickly and without question your officers in the Lord, if you wish to remain a member of this Team, "giving cheerfully, as unto the Lord," "without murmuring," remembering that "Greater love hath no man than this, that he lay down his life for his friends." "Hereby perceive we the love of God: because he laid down his life for us, and we ought to lay down our lives for the brethren." "To love God, and our neighbor as ourselves . . . is all the law."

B. Sociological Survey, Youth for Truth Center, Sacramento, California

The expanded and accelerated education of the 1960's has created a generation of young people wanting to discover their own solutions to existing problems. Many of today's youth have rejected the established answers and methods of carrying out solutions to the serious problems facing the U.S.A. and the world. The young person often finds himself alienated from his parents or society in general because of the choice of methods practiced in discovering hoped-for solutions to personal or social problems. What are some of these more common methods? Drugs, intellectualism, pseudo-freedom, peace movements, Black or Brown Power, race and campus riots, astrology and other forms of white witchcraft, black witchcraft, Eastern thought, spiritualism, and astro-projection. Many young people, finding their way to the Youth for Truth Outreach, are in this condition. This condition is labeled as being at odds with their family or society. Those who still have emotional or financial support from their families are in unity with their families, the conflicts having been resolved.

FAMILY STATUS OF RESIDENTS

Of 55 cases:
Number of people who were at odds with families before
    YFTC program   41 (71%)

Of 41 cases at odds
Number of people united with families as result of YFTC
    program   28 (68%)
Number of people who were in unity with families before
    YFTC program   14 (29%)
Number of people still at odds with family after YFTC
    program   13 (32%)
Number of people who were still at odds with family,
    but successfully completed YFTC program   11
    (Their families rejected them for differences in religious views and for various other reasons.)

Economic Status of Families	*Religious training*	*Present trend*
Upper 1	Ass. of God 7	Agnostic 2
Upper middle ... 3	Baptist 8	Atheist 2
Middle 37	Catholic 15	Buddhist 1
Lower middle ... 2	Lutheran 2	Eastern, gen. 5
Lower 11	Methodist 2	Yoga 4
	Presbyterian 1	Meditation 2
	Covenant 1	
	Protestant, gen. ...17	
	None 1	

Political Point of View

Conservative/Right Wing	 7
Left Wing	15
Liberal	 7
Communist	 1
Women's Lib.	 6
Black Power	10
Brown Power	 4
None	 8

Drug Abuse

Heavy	34
Moderate	 5
Mild	10
Average Length of Involvement	2–3 yrs.
Longest Involvement	8–10 yrs.

Law Violation

Probation 12	Runaways 3	Record Unknown .. 3
Parole 2	Curfew Violations ...2	No Violation 24
Convictions ..12	Boy's Ranch 4	
(Not identified)	C.Y.A. 0	
	Preston Reform 2	

YFTC Rehabilitation Program

Total residents (average age 20 yrs. 3 mos.) 54
Number granted residence 44
Number left in good standing 26
Number left in bad standing 8
Number left before three-week probation period ended .. 9
Number of residents that came to YFTC on the staff 10

Sex and Racial Breakdown

Total percentages

Blacks:	32%	Males:	33 (61%)	Blacks:	14 (42%)
Whites:	57%			Whites:	14 (42%)
Mex-Amer.:	7%			Mex-Amer:	3 (9%)
Latins:	4%			Latins:	2 (7%)
		Females:	21 (39%)	Blacks:	3 (14%)
				Whites:	17 (86%)
				Mex-Amer:	1 (1%)

Monthly Arrivals and Departures

January:	Arrived 4 Left 1	July:	Arrived 6 Left 5
February:	Arrived 3 Left 3	August	Arrived 4 Left 3
March:	Arrived 1 Left 2	September:	Arrived 2 Left 4
April:	Arrived 2 Left 3	October:	Arrived 8 Left 5
May:	Arrived 1 Left 2	November:	Arrived 5 Left 4
June:	Arrived 4 Left 2	December:	Arrived 3 Left 5

Staff worker's average stay: 8 mos. 2 wks.
Resident's average stay: 3 mos.

Drug Abuse

Types of drugs used

1. Hallucinogens 37 (69%)
   LSD, acid, peyote, STP, mescaline, cap, tab, weges,
   swirls, sunshine, orange, purple, osley, chocolate
   chips, etc.
2. Heroin 4 (7%)
   Snow, stuff, H, junk, smack, etc.
3. Methamphetamine 13 (25%)
   Speed, crystal, meth
4. Cocaine 4 (7%)
   Leaf, snow, speedballs
5. Amphetamine 14 (26%)
   Bennies, co-pilots, whites, footballs, pep pills, dexies,
   diet pills, uppers, form of speed
6. Codeine 3 (6%)
   Schoolboy
7. Barbiturates 22 (41%)
   Reds, red birds, yellow jackets, blue heavens, goof
   balls, downers, rainbows
8. Alcohol 9 (17%)
   Cocktails, drinks

Quantity			*Length*	
Heavy	34	(64%)	Average involvement .	2–3 yrs.
Moderate	5	(9%)	Longest involvement .	8–10 yrs.
Mild	10	(19%)		
None	5	(9%)		

REASON FOR COMING TO YFTC

Residents came to YFTC with varied problems; some had more than one major problem. Because of this, many of the following statistics are overlapping.

Family Crisis ..	8	(15%)	Assigned to YFTC on:		
Emotional	34	(64%)	Parole	2	(4%)
Drugs	18	(33%)	Probation	12	(22%)
Rebellion	13	(25%)	Run-aways	3	(6%)
Spaced Mind ...	8	(15%)	(Under-age; returned home)		
Health and					
Rehabilitation .	1				

(Referred by doctor to recover from effects of hepatitis)

YFTC is a home providing Christian outlook and values on life. Nineteen residents (35%) came to the center for Personal Growth. Their environment did not provide the guidance in Christian training that was needed to gain a strong foundation to build a changed life on.

Bibliography

BOOKS

BLESSITT, ARTHUR, *Turned On to Jesus.* New York: Hawthorne, 1971.

BRESHEARS, ARLENE, ed., *Psalter.* Long Beach, Calif.: Bethany Missionary Association.

——, ed. *Jesus People Hymnal.* Vancouver, British Columbia: St. Margaret's Episcopal Reformed Church.

CANNON, WILLIAM S., *The Jesus Revolution.* Nashville: Broadman, 1971.

EASTMAN, DICK, *Up With Jesus.* Grand Rapids: Baker, 1971.

ENROTH, RONALD M.; ERICKSON, EDWARD E., JR., and PETERS, C. BRECKINRIDGE, *The Jesus People: Old-Time Religion in the Age of Aquarius.* Grand Rapids: Eerdmans, 1972.

EVANS, ROBERT A., *Belief and the Counter Culture.* (Philadelphia: Westminster, 1971.

FITZGERALD, GEORGE R., *Communes: Their Goals, Hopes, Problems.* Glen Rock, N.J., 1971.

FORD, CLAY, *Berkeley Journal: Jesus and the Street People—A Firsthand Report,* New York: Harper & Row, 1971.

GOLD, ROBERT S., *The Rebel Culture.* New York: Dell, 1970.

GRAHAM, BILLY, *The Jesus Generation.* Grand Rapids: Zondervan, 1971.

GRIERSON, DENHAM, *Young People in Communal Living.* Philadelphia: Westminster, 1971.

HANNA, THOMAS, *Bodies in Revolt.* New York: Holt, Rinehart, and Winston, 1971.

JOHNSTON, WILLIAM, *Christian Zen.* New York: Harper and Row, 1971.

KNIGHT, WALKER L., *Jesus People Come Alive*. Wheaton, Ill.: Tyndale, 1971.

KOCH, KURT, *Between Christ and Satan, the Devil's Alphabet*. Grand Rapids: Kregel, 1971.

LIFTON, ROBERT JAY, *Boundaries: Psychological Man in Revolution*. New York: Random, 1971.

LINDSEY, HAL, with C. C. CARLSON, *The Late Great Planet Earth*. Grand Rapids: Zondervan, 1970.

MACDONALD, JOHN A., *House of Acts*. Creation House: 1970.

MARCINIAK, ED, *Tomorrow's Christian*. Dayton, O.: Pflaum, 1969.

MOODY, JESS, *The Jesus Freaks*. Waco, Texas: Word, 1971.

MUDGE, LEWIS, *The Crumbling Walls*. Philadelphia: Westminster, 1970.

NEE, WATCHMAN, *Changed Into His Likeness*. Fort Washington, Pa.: Christian Literature Crusade, 1967.

————, *Further Talks on the Church Life*. Los Angeles: Stream Publishers, 1969.

NEFF, H. RICHARD, *Psychic Phenomena and Religion*. (Philadelphia: Westminster, 1971.

PALMQUIST, ALLEN, and REYNOLDS, FRANK, *The Drug Bug*, with foreword by David Wilkerson. Minneapolis: Bethany Fellowship, 1970.

PALMS, ROGER C., *The Jesus Kids*. Valley Forge, Pa.: Judson Press, 1971.

PEDERSON, DUANE, *Jesus People*. Pasadena, Calif.: Compass Press, 1971.

ORTEGA, RUBEN, *The Jesus People Speak Out*. Elgin. Ill.: David C. Cook, 1971.

PLOWMAN, EDWARD E., *The Underground Church* (renamed in later editions, *The Jesus People Movement in the U.S.*). Elgin: David C. Cook Co., 1971.

REES, D. VAUGHAN, *The "Jesus Family" in Communist China*. Exeter, England: Paternoster Press, c. 1959. Third edition, 1967.

REICH, CHARLES, *The Greening of America*. New York: Random House, 1970.

ROSZAK, THEODORE, *The Making of a Counter Culture*. New York: Doubleday, 1969.

SHERRILL, JOHN L., *They Speak With Other Tongues*. New York: Pyramid Books, 1964, 1970.

SMITH, ELWYN A., ed., *What the Religious Revolutionaries Are Saying*. Philadelphia: Fortress, 1971.

STRUCHEN, JEANETTE, *Zapped by Jesus*. New York: J. B. Lippincott Co., 1972.

SYNAN, VINSON, *The Holiness-Pentecostal Movement in the United States*. Grand Rapids: Eerdman's, 1971.

STREIKER, LOWELL D., *The Jesus Trip: Advent of the Jesus Freaks*. Nashville: Abingdon, 1971.

Two Brothers From Berkeley, *Letters to Street Christians.* Grand Rapids: Zondervan, 1971.

Ward, Hiley H., *Rock 2000.* Nashville: Abingdon, 1969.

Webber, Robert, ed., *Rappings.* Wheaton: Tyndale, 1971.

Wierville, Victor Paul, *Are the Dead Alive Now?* Old Greenwich, Conn.: Devin-Adair, 1971.

Wilkerson, David and Don, *The Untapped Generation.* Grand Rapids: Zondervan, 1971.

———, *Jesus Person Maturity Manual.* Glendale, Calif.: Regal Books, 1971.

Wood, Barry, *The Magnificent Frolic.* Philadelphia: Westminster, 1970.

Wright, J. Stafford, *Mind, Man and the Spirits.* (Grand Rapids: Zondervan, 1971.

MAGAZINES

Action, McKenna, David, "Are Jesus Kids Joel's Children?—An Evangelical Analysis of the Jesus Movement," Fall, 1971, p. 9–14.

America, Campion, Donald, ex. ed., "Youth 'Liberates' America," special report, Apr. 25, 1970, p. 429ff; Rule, Philip C., "The Decline of Flower Power," Feb. 13, 1971, pp. 141–145; Haughey, John C., "The Commune—Child of the 1970's," Mar. 13, 1971, pp. 254ff; O'Collins, Gerald, "The Greening of Christianity," April 17, 1971, p. 410; Conway, James F., "New Turn on Campus—The Christian Commune," May 8, 1971, pp. 479–481; Donnelly, Doris, "Jesus and the Star System," Oct. 30, 1971; Gelpi, Donald, "Religion in the Age of Aquarius," Nov. 13, 1971, pp. 392–5.

Christian Century, Hacker, Helen M., "How Clergymen View Hippiedom," July 22, 1970, pp. 887–890; Fager, Charles, "An Interview with Harvey Cox—Experimenting with a Simpler Life Style," Jan. 6, 1971, pp. 9–13; Fackre, Gabriel, "Going East: Neomysticism and Christian Faith," April 14, 1971, pp. 457–461; editorial, "Now That Jesus Is 'In' Again," June 23, 1971, p. 767.

Christianity Today, Klein, Rita, "Spiritual Revolution—West Coast Youth," June 19, 1970, p. 876; Plowman, Edward E., "Revival in the 'Underground'—Pacific Northwest," Jan. 29, 1971, pp. 430–31; "Jesus Freaks Move Right On," Mar. 12, 1971, p. 569; "Followers of the Way," Mar. 26, 1971, pp. 618–19; "Jesus Presses Are Rolling," Apr. 9, 1971, p. 664; "Shore to Shore: Wave of Witness," beach scene, May 7, 1971, pp. 34–35; "The Jesus Movement: Now It's in the Hamlets," June 18, 1971, pp. 903, 904; Eggerbrotten, Anne, "Jesus Festivals," Aug. 6, 1971, pp. 1022–1024; Williams, Donald M., "Close-up of the Jesus People," Aug. 27, 1971, pp. 1033–1035; special report, "Where Have All the Children Gone?" Report on the Children of God, Nov. 5, 1971, pp. 146–148.

Commonweal, Bloy, Myron B., Jr., "Culture and Counter-Culture—Alienated Youth's Risky Challenge to the Establishment," Jan. 17, 1969, pp. 493–496; Tracy, Phil, "The Jesus Freaks—Savagery and Salvation on Sunset Strip," Oct. 30, 1970, pp. 122–125.

Life, "The Groovy Christians of Rye, N.Y.," May 14, 1971.

Look, Cheetham, Jack and Betty, "The Jesus Movement Is Upon Us," Feb. 9, 1971, pp. 15–21.

Newsweek, "Generation Gap," Children of God, Nov. 22, 1971, pp. 89, 90.

Ramparts, Nolan, James, "Jesus Now: Hogwash and Holy Water," Aug. 1971, pp. 18–26.

Time, cover story on "The Jesus Revolution," with color pictures, June 21, 1971, pp. 56–63.

NEWSPAPERS

Christian Science Monitor, Sterritt, David, "Rock Finds Religion," Mar. 10, 1971.

New York Times, Fiske, Edward, "New Youth Groups 'Freaked Out' on Jesus" (San Francisco), 1970; Kovach, Bill, "Communes Spread as the Young Reject Old Values," Dec. 17, 1970; King, Seth S., "New Religious Communities: Alternative to Life in Convent," Feb. 16, 1971; Fiske, " 'Jesus People' Are Happy With Their Life in Love Inn" (Freeville, N.Y.), June 14, 1971; Currivan, Gene, " 'Jesus Groups' Conduct 'Spiritual Revolution' at UN," June 27, 1971; Fiske, Edward, "Jesus People: In a Good Old American Tradition," July 4, 1971; Wooten, James, "Ill Winds Buffet Communal Sect," Nov. 29, 1971; Kneeland, Douglas E., "The Jesus Movement Spreading on Campus" (Palo Alto, Calif.), Dec. 25, 1971; Blau, Eleanor, "Children of God Return Home From Visits to Rejected Past," Jan. 17, 1972.

Wall Street Journal, Gottschalk, Jr., Earl C., "Hip Culture Discovers a New Trip: Fervent, Foot-Stompin' Religion," Mar. 2, 1971.

Index